Elite • 126

Siege Warfare in the Roman World

146 BC–AD 378

Duncan B Campbell • Illustrated by Adam Hook

Consultant editor Martin Windrow

First published in Great Britain in 2005 by Osprey Publishing
Elms Court, Chapel Way, Botley, Oxford OX2 9LP, United Kingdom
Email: **info@ospreypublishing.com**

CIP data for this publication is available from the British Library.

ISBN 1 84176 782 4

Consultant Editor: Martin Windrow
Editor: Ruth Sheppard
Design: Ken Vail Graphic Design, Cambridge, UK
Index by Glyn Sutcliffe
Originated by PPS Grasmere, Leeds, UK
Printed in China through World Print Ltd.

05 06 07 08 09   10 9 8 7 6 5 4 3 2 1

FOR A CATALOGUE OF ALL BOOKS PUBLISHED BY
OSPREY MILITARY AND AVIATION PLEASE CONTACT:

The Marketing Manager, Osprey Direct UK
PO Box 140, Wellingborough, Northants NN8 2FA, United Kingdom
Email: **info@ospreydirect.co.uk**

NORTH AMERICA
Osprey Direct, 2427 Bond Street, University Park, IL 60466, USA
Email: **info@ospreydirectusa.com**

www.ospreypublishing.com

Dedication

In memory of my father, William Robertson Campbell, who passed away during the writing of this book.
Estin de pistis elpizomenōn hupostasis… (Heb. 11.1)

Acknowledgements

It is again a pleasure to acknowledge the generosity of colleagues who provided illustrations for this book, or assisted in their supply. Most are acknowledged in the photo captions, except: Chris Haines (Ermine Street Guard), Michael E. Moss (West Point Museum), Stephen Ressler (US Military Academy, West Point), Véronique Brouquier-Reddé and David Woolliscroft.

Author's Note

All ancient sources are referenced using the abbreviations recommended by *The Oxford Classical Dictionary*. All translations are my own.

Artist's Note

Readers may care to note that the original paintings from which the colour plates in this book were prepared are available for private sale. All reproduction copyright whatsoever is retained by the Publishers. All enquiries should be addressed to:

Scorpio Gallery, PO Box 475, Hailsham, East Sussex BN27 2SL, UK

The Publishers regret that they can enter into no correspondence upon this matter.

SIEGE WARFARE IN THE ROMAN WORLD 146 BC–AD 378

INTRODUCTION

In the decades following the defeat of Hannibal in 202 BC, various conflicts took Roman armies far and wide around the Mediterranean. The siege warfare that they practised largely took the form of the storming assault. But Rome's acquaintance with Macedon, as both adversary and ally, perhaps opened the eyes of her generals to the possibilities of more sophisticated tactics. P. Sulpicius Galba, attempting to raise Philip V's siege of Echinus in 210 BC, could not have failed to have been impressed by the Macedonian siege train.[1] Twenty years later, M'. Acilius Glabrio deployed substantially the same kind of machinery outside the Greek town of Heraclea. For 24 days, his men persevered with 'siege towers, battering rams, and all the other equipment for besieging a town' (Livy 36.22.9), before they were finally unleashed in a terrifying escalade.

Circumstances had not changed by the time of the fall of Carthage, half a century later. The surest tactic for capturing fortified positions remained the storming assault, which Roman armies appear to have conducted with particular ferocity. The increasingly common employment of machinery did not guarantee success, a fact that perhaps indicates a general absence of artillery to provide covering fire. In 148 BC, for example, at Hippagreta near Carthage, L. Calpurnius Piso is said to have spent all summer attempting to break into the town, but the defenders persisted in burning his siege machines (App., *Pun.* 110). Wooden machinery was always

---

1. See Elite 121: *Ancient Siege Warfare: Persians, Greeks, Carthaginians and Romans 546–146 BC*, plate F and p. 63.

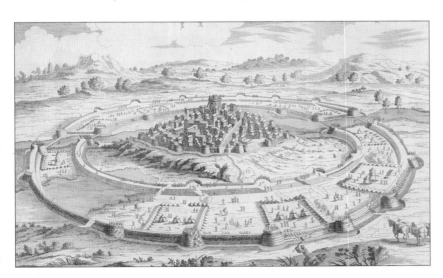

The 18th-century Chevalier de Folard's engraving of Numantia displays no geographical knowledge of the site and little consideration of Appian's description, but demonstrates how de Folard's contemporaries imagined a typical Roman siege. The mistaken belief that Roman armies invariably attempted to blockade their enemies was still common into the 20th century. (Author's collection)

Herod the Great built a fortified palace at Herodium (near Bethlehem, Israel), crowning a conical hill. The place was equipped to withstand siege. Prominent among its defensive arsenal were dozens of large worked boulders, designed to be rolled down the hillside onto any attackers. (© Author)

susceptible to burning; this is a theme that all siegecraft writers return to, again and again. However, in later ages, artillery and missile troops were deployed to provide the continuous bombardment which discouraged such incendiary attacks. At Hippagreta, Piso gave up, where a better general would perhaps have persevered.

Events at Carthage neatly encapsulate Roman siegecraft of the period. The consuls of 149 BC, ignorant of the fact that the demilitarised city was actively re-arming, rashly assumed that she would easily fall to escalade. When several attempts failed, they settled down to construct siege machinery. Appian records the construction of 'two enormous ram-carrying machines' (App., *Pun.* 98), allegedly crewed by 6,000 men; their deployment required the consolidation of a pathway along the edge of the stagnant Lake of Tunis, which implies that they were targeted at the city's south wall. The attempt was frustrated, however, when the defenders not only repaired any wall breaches that the Romans managed to make, but also crept out by night and set the machines ablaze. Nothing was achieved in this first year of the siege, and in the second the Romans concentrated on Carthage's allies in the north African hinterland. In the third year, 147 BC, a mishandled escalade resulted in several thousand Romans being pinned down in an area just inside the city; they were extricated only by the timely arrival of Scipio Aemilianus, who was due to take up the command in 146.

Scipio restored the men's flagging morale by mounting a raid on the leafy Megara district of Carthage. Then, reviving a strategy from past generations, he proceeded to isolate the city by imposing a blockade. None of the great sieges within recent memory had utilised such a strategy. But as the adopted grandson of the great Scipio Africanus, he must have heard the story of Orongis, besieged by Africanus' brother in 207 BC; here, the town had been ringed with a double ditch and rampart, before being subjected to full-scale assault (Livy 28.3.2–16). Scipio had something similar in mind for Carthage.

First, he cut the city's land communications with a huge earthwork that simultaneously sealed the 4½km-wide isthmus and provided shelter for the Roman siege troops.[2] Then, he blocked the great harbour, Carthage's lifeline to the Mediterranean, by constructing a mole across the entrance. With the city isolated, the assault could commence,

2. See Elite 121: *Ancient Siege Warfare: Persians, Greeks, Carthaginians and Romans 546–146 BC*, plate G and p. 63.

and Scipio brought up battering rams to break down the quay wall. In desperation, some of the Carthaginians swam across the harbour to set fire to the Roman machinery, while others attempted to fortify the quay but were repulsed with horrendous loss of life. Appian (perhaps quoting the eyewitness report of Polybius) claims that 'the walkway was so slippery with blood, freshly and copiously spilled, that [the Romans] reluctantly abandoned the pursuit of those who were fleeing' (App., *Pun.* 125). It only remained to launch the storming assault, which had sealed the fate of so many of Rome's adversaries, and after six days of destruction the city lay in ruins.

SIEGE WARFARE IN THE LATE SECOND CENTURY BC

The Eastern Mediterranean, 163–133 BC

A generation or two earlier, Rome had become embroiled in the affairs of Macedon and Greece, and gradually imposed her authority on both. From there, it was a short step to Asia Minor, but for the time being, the Romans studiously avoided military involvement farther east. However, warfare continued in her absence, notably in Judaea, where Judas Maccabaeus led the Hasmonean revolt against Seleucid overlordship. In 163 BC, he besieged the citadel at Jerusalem, the so-called Akra, and expelled the garrison. It is clear that the siegecraft practised by the Jewish forces was fully developed: the historian Josephus reports that Judas 'prepared machinery and raised embankments' (*AJ* 12.363), while

The Mediterranean world, showing some sites besieged during the period 146–27 BC. (© Author)

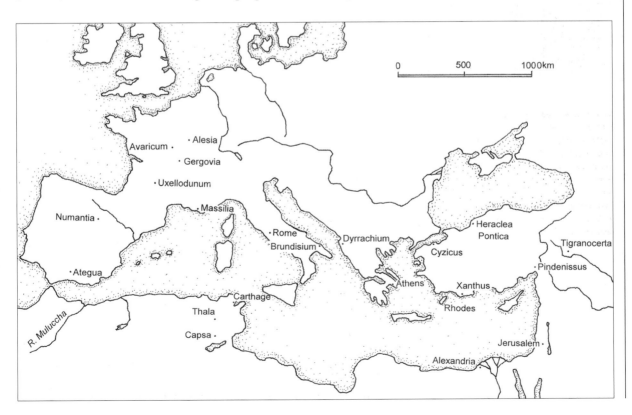

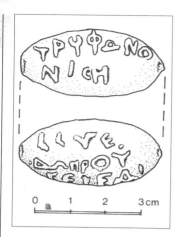

A sling bullet from Tel Dor, Israel, inscribed in Greek, announcing 'Tryphon's victory' (*Tryphōno(s) nikē*, lines 1–2). The remainder of the message is unclear. However, it was common practice to inscribe taunting insults on sling bullets, and the final line was perhaps intended to read 'Have a taste!' (*geusai*). (© Author)

Stone balls discovered near the eastern (landward) gate of Tel Dor. The smooth, carefully dressed stones, ranging from 1kg to 26kg, were clearly designed for use by stone-projecting catapults. Some are inscribed with an approximation of their weight. (© I. Shatzman, by courtesy of Prof. E. Stern and the Tel Dor Project)

an earlier account emphasises the use of 'artillery emplacements and machines' (*1 Macc.* 6.20). When the conflict flared up again in the 140s BC, Judas' brother Jonathan 'brought up many siege machines' against the Akra (*1 Macc.* 11.20), while Simon besieged Beth-Sura, one of the main centres of Seleucid power in Judaea; the rapid construction of embankments and machinery threw the garrison into a panic, and they withdrew under truce (Joseph., *AJ* 13.156). Later, at the siege of Gazara, Simon 'constructed a *helepolis* and brought it up to the town, battered a tower, and captured it'; the fact that 'the men in the *helepolis* leapt out into the town' (*1 Macc.* 13.43–4) suggests that it was designed like a siege tower, but the machine clearly incorporated a battering ram.

Jonathan was later killed by the Seleucid pretender Tryphon, who was in turn besieged by the rightful king, Antiochus VII, in the coastal town of Dora (Tel Dor in Israel) in 138 BC. The Seleucid forces encircled the town to prevent any escape, and proceeded to attack the walls with machinery. However, Tryphon did not wait to see the outcome, preferring to flee by ship to Apamea, where he met his end. Excavations at Tel Dor throughout the 1980s unearthed sling bullets, arrowheads and the rounded stone balls used by catapults,[3] as well as larger ones which must have been intended for rolling. Antiochus VII's campaign to reconquer Judaea ultimately brought him to Jerusalem, which he surrounded with two deep, wide ditches, seven camps, and a hundred three-storey towers (Joseph., *AJ* 13.238–9); the city was starved into submission, despite the defenders' attempt to expel all who could not contribute to the defence.

Rome's Spanish campaigns, 153–134 BC

All this time, Roman armies were busy in Spain, where the defeat of the Carthaginians had left a vacuum. In 195 BC, M. Porcius Cato achieved great successes in the south, but when he claimed to have captured four hundred 'towns' (Plut., *Cato Mai.* 10.3) he perhaps used the term loosely. Similarly, in 181 BC, Q. Fulvius Flaccus was said to have captured 'many forts' there (Livy 40.33.9). At any rate, Roman campaigns among the Celtiberians of the northern highlands succeeded only in stirring up a resentment that would last for generations. In 153 BC, Q. Fulvius Nobilior, whose father had besieged Ambracia in 189 BC,[4] attempted to capture the Celtiberian stronghold of Numantia, but failure forced his successor to conclude a peace treaty. In 142 BC, it was the turn of Q. Caecilius Metellus, who had earned the sobriquet 'Macedonicus' from his success against rebels in northern Greece. His term of office is chiefly remembered for events at two Celtiberian towns. First, in the vicinity of Contrebia, Metellus devised the stratagem of marching and counter-marching in a desultory fashion until the townsfolk grew complacent, at which point he descended upon them suddenly and captured

3. See New Vanguard 89: *Greek and Roman Artillery 399 BC–AD 363*, pp. 20–21.
4. See Elite 121: *Ancient Siege Warfare: Persians, Greeks, Carthaginians and Romans 546–146 BC*, pp. 55–56.

View from the hill town of Numantia (Spain), looking north. To the right lies the site of the camp at Castillejo, and to the left is the hill of Alto Real; the confluence of the rivers Duero and Tera is in the centre of the picture. (© F. Quesada)

the town by surprise (Val. Max. 7.4.5). He insisted upon such secrecy that not even his officers were aware of his intentions, giving rise to the story that, when asked for the next day's orders, Metellus responded, 'if my own tunic could tell, I would burn it' (Frontin., *Str.* 1.1.12).

The second town was Centobriga, and here Metellus deployed siege machinery. The writer Valerius Maximus, who compiled his *Memorable Words and Deeds* for the emperor Tiberius around AD 30, records that the defenders seized the children of a deserter and 'exposed them to the blows of the machine' (Val. Max. 5.1.5). Metellus immediately broke off the assault to spare the boys' lives, whereupon the neighbouring communities bowed to Rome, apparently overawed by Metellus' honour and clemency. Valerius Maximus seems to imply that the Romans were using a battering ram. But Livy's version of the story specifies that 'the people of Centobriga exposed the children of the deserter Rethogenes to the shots of the artillery' (Livy, *Per.* 53). It is true that Valerius Maximus is often criticised for inaccuracy, but it is conceivable that, on this occasion, both he and Livy are correct, if the Roman battering assault was accompanied by an artillery barrage.

Meanwhile, Numantia continued to defy Rome. Admittedly, the hilltop site was difficult to approach, but the historian Velleius Paterculus (a source far superior to his contemporary Valerius Maximus) could not decide whether the Numantine success was due to native courage or Roman incompetence (Vell. Pat. 2.1.4). Metellus' successor, Q. Pompeius, resorted to diverting the town's water supply (App., *Hisp.* 78), but his men were constantly harassed as they worked, and new recruits sent out to replace losses fell ill and died from dysentery. In order to conceal the failure of a campaign marked by defeat and humiliation, Pompeius made a pact with the townsfolk, but almost immediately reneged. It was left to his successor, M. Popillius Laenas, to continue the war in 138 BC. This time, the Numantines were determined to remain within their fortifications, so Laenas tried escalade. However, it seems that, fearing a trap, he cancelled the assault at the last moment, exposing his retreating troops to attack in the rear and subjecting Rome to yet another humiliating defeat (Frontin., *Str.* 3.17.9). His successor's year of office, 137 BC, was likewise marked by misfortune and defeat. Indeed, matters were so bad that C. Hostilius Mancinus abandoned camp and prepared to withdraw by night, but the Numantines pressed his retreating army so hard that he sued for peace (Plut., *Ti. Gracch.* 5.1–4). The Senate in Rome subsequently refused to ratify such a humiliating pact, and even sent Mancinus back to the Numantines, in symbolic cancellation of the treaty.

Meanwhile, Mancinus' successor, M. Aemilius Lepidus Porcina, turned his attention to the town of Pallantia. However, despite the use of siege machines, operations dragged on so long that the Romans again fell foul of famine and disease, the bane of any army making a lengthy stay on the same spot. Lepidus was forced to adopt Mancinus' reprehensible tactics, and withdrew under cover of darkness, leaving the sick and wounded behind. He was subsequently recalled to Rome and fined (App., *Hisp.* 82–3). His replacement, Q. Calpurnius Piso, avoided Numantia altogether, preferring to take a small amount of plunder from the exhausted Pallantines.

The siege of Numantia, 133 BC

Such was the catalogue of disasters facing Scipio Aemilianus, the destroyer of Carthage, when he arrived at Numantia. The friends and clients with whom he travelled perhaps included Polybius; although this historian's work terminated with the events of 146 BC, he was a companion of Scipio's, and is widely presumed to have been the ultimate source for Appian's description of the Numantine campaign.

In a move which was entirely characteristic of Roman warfare, operations began with the siting of a camp some distance from the town, before the troops moved up for the siege (App., *Hisp.* 87). This camp may have been one of the five which the German archaeologist Adolf Schulten found 7km east of Numantia on the hill of Renieblas, but the chronology of the site has never been adequately untangled. Having reconnoitred from afar, Scipio then established two camps outside the town, one under his own command and the other under his brother, Q. Fabius Maximus (App., *Hisp.* 90). Schulten's intimate knowledge of the site, from excavations conducted in the area between 1905 and 1912, led him to place Scipio at Castillejo, a hill to the north of the town; Maximus he placed to the south, on the hill of Peña Redonda. His conjectures stemmed partly from an appreciation of the topography, and there is no denying that Castillejo occupies the prime strategic position, separated from the town by a kilometre

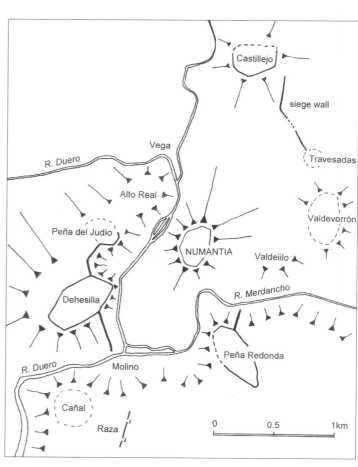

Plan of Numantia, showing the locations mentioned in the text. (© Author)

View from Peña Redonda, looking west towards the hill of Cañal. The ruins of the Roman camp can be seen in the foreground, while on the right, the winding course of the Merdancho can be seen (marked *b*). The distant hill on the right is Dehesilla. (A. Schulten, *Numantia: Die Ergebnisse der Ausgrabungen 1905–1912*, vol. III: *Die Lager des Scipio*, Munich 1927)

of rolling countryside. But there is no particular reason to place Maximus at Peña Redonda. Its inaccessible location ensured that the archaeological remains survived relatively undisturbed, and the degree of preservation may have clouded Schulten's judgement. The big camp at Dehesilla is a better candidate, commanding an altogether easier approach to Numantia and providing an overview of the western side to complement Castillejo's control of the north and east.

His predecessors had tried every stratagem known to them, so Scipio settled on the construction of an ambitious set of siege-works. Appian describes a sequence comprising the initial two camps, followed by the siting of seven forts around the town; then, because the nearby river Duero could not be bridged, 'he set two forts alongside it' as the anchor points for floating obstacles (App., *Hisp.* 91). Besides Castillejo, Peña Redonda and Dehesilla, Schulten identified another four, far less well-preserved camps, to arrive at a total of seven, and postulated a further two 'riverbank forts'; this scheme has remained largely uncontested.

There can be little doubt that a 7ha siege camp sat on the hill at Castillejo; besides sporadic remains of limestone foundations, corresponding to barracks and possibly a headquarters building, there were finds of Roman pottery, coins and weaponry. Similarly, at Peña Redonda, the outline of an 11ha camp is clearly marked by the foundations of a 4m-thick stone rampart; extensive remains of barracks and other buildings can still be seen, and the site produced the same kind of finds as at Castillejo. South of Castillejo and about half a kilometre due east of Numantia, Schulten postulated a camp on the low hill of Valdevorrón. Although a perimeter rampart was not located, the site turned up ceramic evidence and some small finds including a Roman coin; the terrain would have permitted a camp of up to 9ha. The sizeable gap to the north was closed by a camp at Travesadas, situated on a 4ha plot of low-lying ground. Here, the remains of buildings and sporadic traces of the defences were unearthed, along with pottery and small finds. Schulten also found pottery and traces of stonework on the hill of Valdelilo, but he considered its position dangerously close to Numantia, so he excluded it from consideration.

Schulten believed that Scipio must have placed a garrison at the southern end of Numantia, but all he found on the hill of Raza was a 300m stretch of wall with two *titulus*-protected gates.[5] More recent field-work there failed to recover any archaeological material whatsoever, but Spanish researchers have reported ceramic evidence and possible traces of defences on the neighbouring hill of Cañal, which commands views over the entire siege complex. Clearer evidence was found on the riverside at

View towards Peña Redonda from the hill of Numantia, taken in early morning sunshine. The siege wall descends the slope on the left (running from *d* to *e*), from the Roman camp down to the river. (A. Schulten, *Numantia: Die Ergebnisse der Ausgrabungen 1905–1912*, vol. III: *Die Lager des Scipio*, Munich 1927)

Molino, where the foundations of one or two possible barracks were found, along with pottery and small finds including a Roman dagger. Schulten took these to be evidence of a small fort, and identified a second one further north at Vega, where the remains were far less coherent but the tell-tale pottery pointed to a Roman presence. Curiously, Schulten treated these two 'riverbank forts' separately from his main series of seven camps. Vega, of course, would have been an ideal spot for Scipio's river-blocking measures, at the confluence of the rivers Duero and Tera; a barrier here would have caught any supplies before they drifted down past the town.[6]

Schulten was confident that a camp lay on Alto Real, a low hill overlooking Vega, but he found only tumbledown walling and, despite small quantities of pottery, it is debatable whether one of Scipio's forts stood here. (Interestingly, Schulten pronounced that the remains were unworthy of Roman workmanship, and could only have been built by Iberian auxiliaries!) By contrast, there can be no doubt about the remains at Dehesilla; although ploughing had destroyed the interior, Schulten was able to trace the complete perimeter of a 14ha enclosure. Between the two, on the hill of Peña del Judío, he suggested the siting of a tower, but wall foundations were found curving around the hill in a suggestive manner, and the associated pottery scatter holds out the possibility of an enclosure of up to 4ha.

Scipio's siege-works consisted of more than just camps and forts. Appian notes that 'here Scipio first, I suppose, enclosed a town which did not refuse open battle' (*Hisp.* 91). In fact, this was precisely the tactic he had used at Carthage, again as a last resort. (In claiming an innovation at Numantia, Appian is perhaps conscious of the fact that Carthage was not strictly 'enclosed', but cut off; also, unlike the Numantines, her defenders had been in no hurry to take the field against Rome.) Appian

RIGHT **One of Schulten's excavation trenches south of Dehesilla, looking downhill towards Molino. Some of the stones forming the foundations of Scipio's siege wall measured almost 1 cubic metre. (A. Schulten, *Numantia: Die Ergebnisse der Ausgrabungen 1905–1912*, vol. III: *Die Lager des Scipio*, Munich 1927)**

---

5. *Titulus* is the name given to a length of rampart and ditch lying some distance outside a gap in the defences; this was the standard Roman method of protecting an open gateway.
6. In fact, Schulten proposed two river barriers, at Vega and Molino, but Appian's description is ambiguous; he could mean two forts, opposite one another, supporting a single barrier.

View from the north side of Dehesilla (marked *c*), looking towards Castillejo (*a*). Schulten discovered the line of Scipio's siege wall as it crosses Peña del Judío (*b*). (A. Schulten, *Numantia: Die Ergebnisse der Ausgrabungen 1905–1912*, vol. III: *Die Lager des Scipio*, Munich 1927)

relates that Scipio proceeded to surround Numantia with a ditch and palisade, then another ditch not far behind, and finally a wall 8ft wide and 10ft high (2.4 x 3.0m), with towers at intervals of 1 *plethron* (31m). Although Schulten failed to locate any ditch, he found traces of Appian's *periteichismos*, or walled encirclement, at various spots around Numantia. The short length identified between Castillejo and Travesadas was badly ruined, surviving only as a limestone facing with a metre of rubble backing. However, a substantial length was uncovered on either side of Dehesilla, where it was found to comprise an inner and an outer stone facing, sandwiching a rough, stony infill; the overall width was approximately 3.5m. And on the stretch running up to Peña Redonda,

an extra layer had been added to the sandwich, resulting in an overall width of 4.7m. Schulten reasoned that, from these massive foundations, the wall must have been stepped at the rear, in order to arrive at a 2.4m-wide wallwalk (corresponding to Appian's reported width of 8ft). He calculated that a complete circuit would have measured around 9km; but, as the stretches he uncovered totalled only 1,680m, it may be that other parts were never built in stone. The absence of a ditch he explained by reference to the rivers, proposing that it had only ever existed on the eastern side, where there was no river to screen the siege-works.

Only limited traces of Appian's interval towers were found. First, south of Dehesilla, Schulten thought he could discern a trio of 3m-wide

11

guard rooms tacked onto the rear of the siege wall, and spaced at roughly 25m intervals. However, the remains are rather ephemeral. Another pair of similar annexes, further south near Molino, was better preserved. But more striking were the massive, stone-revetted post-holes which Schulten found, immediately behind the siege wall, on the same stretch near Dehesilla. He believed them to be sockets for the corner posts of Appian's watch towers, although no clearly defined set of four came to light. Nevertheless, he decided that, on the Dehesilla–Molino stretch, towers with a floor area of around 5m x 5m were positioned at roughly 8m intervals. For their appearance, Schulten favoured a two-storey timber-built design, with the front uprights buried in the siege wall (see illustration on page 53); but the artillery expert, General Erwin Schramm, preferred the safety of a position entirely behind the wall, where he proposed a freestanding three-storey design, with one or two light catapults above wallwalk level and a signalling mast on the upper floor.

Schulten believed that Scipio constructed a full circumvallation, linking seven camps (Castillejo, Travesadas, Valdevorron, Peña Redonda, Raza, Dehesilla and Alto Real) and two 'river forts' (Vega and Molino). A strict reading of Appian requires two camps, seven forts and another two river barrier forts. We have seen that, of Schulten's proposed sites, Raza probably ought to be replaced by Cañal, and Alto Real by Peña del Judío, while Molino should be raised to the status of a fort; the less substantial remains at Vega might have been linked with Scipio's river barrier. If we designate Castillejo and (arguably) Dehesilla as camps, this leaves only six forts, and it may be that Valdelilo was Scipio's seventh. At any rate, it must be admitted that the archaeology does not sit happily with Appian's description.

A worker stands in one of the post-holes which Schulten discovered on the Numantia siege wall south of Dehesilla. The hole is elliptical, 1.3m long by 0.8m wide and 1.6m deep. Schulten reasoned that the large dimensions were to allow a thick upright timber to be securely wedged in place. (A. Schulten, *Numantia: Die Ergebnisse der Ausgrabungen 1905–1912*, vol. III: *Die Lager des Scipio*, Munich 1927)

SIEGE WARFARE IN THE AGE OF MARIUS AND SULLA

The war against Jugurtha, 111–105 BC

On the death of Micipsa, the philo-Roman ruler of Numidia (north Africa), his adopted son, Jugurtha, challenged the rightful heir, Adherbal, and besieged him in the town of Cirta. The writer Sallust describes how, after an initial assault 'with shelters, towers and machines of all kinds' (*Jug.* 21.3), Jugurtha encircled the town with a ditch and palisade, and erected watch towers. The blockade continued for four months until the townsfolk surrendered, appealing for Roman arbitration. However, Jugurtha took the opportunity to kill his rival and slaughter all the men in the town. Sallust explains that Jugurtha had resorted to blockade 'because its natural strength prevented his taking Cirta by storm' (*Jug.* 23.1). It may be more than coincidental that Jugurtha had served as a Roman ally at Numantia, where he saw Scipio blockade a similarly unassailable town.

When Rome tried to restore order, successive consuls failed to capture Jugurtha, including the nephew of the Metellus who had achieved success in Spain 35 years earlier. (Nevertheless, in the tradition of his family, this Q. Caecilius Metellus took the sobriquet 'Numidicus'.) In 109 BC, he surrounded Zama with pickets of troops and attempted simultaneously to undermine and to scale the walls, under a barrage provided by slingers. But the defence was ferocious: having lined the walls with artillery, the townsfolk rolled down boulders, threw sharpened stakes, and poured a burning mixture of pitch and sulphur onto the Romans. In the following year, at Thala, Metellus surrounded the town with a ditch and palisade, perhaps deliberately emulating Jugurtha's tactic at Cirta. However, he then constructed an embankment to carry battering rams up to the wall and, in the sixth week, broke through the defences. Unfortunately, weeks earlier, Jugurtha had slipped out of the town unnoticed, and the townsfolk, in desperation, burned their valuables and threw themselves onto the bonfire.

Metellus' successor was C. Marius, a 50-year-old soldier of humble origins, who had earlier served with distinction at Numantia. He famously swelled his ranks with the landless poor, placed under the watchful eyes of reliable time-served veterans. After storming several minor towns, just to blood his new troops, he decided to capture the desert town of Capsa, which was 'protected not only by its ramparts and weapons and men, but still more by the difficulty of the surrounding country' (Sall., *Jug.* 89.4). Indeed, the remoteness of some north African towns presented Roman armies with major logistical problems. At Thala, the supply of drinking water had been Metellus' primary concern, until a chance downpour simultaneously solved his difficulties and convinced his troops that they were under divine protection. Similarly, Capsa's inaccessible location demanded special tactics. Marius decided to drive cattle alongside his marching column, so that his troops ate fresh meat for a week and saved the hides to manufacture water skins for their march across the desert. Three days from Capsa, they embarked on a series of night marches with minimal equipment and, when they arrived unexpectedly before the town, they quickly seized the gates. Although the populace promptly surrendered, Marius' troops sacked the place, killing all the adult males. Sallust explains that this was to deny Jugurtha a strong base, and should not be taken to imply greed or brutality on Marius' part.

A second major siege conducted by Marius relied on audacious assault. The target was Jugurtha's treasury, located in an isolated fort on a rocky hill near the Muluccha river. According to Sallust, 'the place was unsuitable for embankments, siege towers, and other machinery' (*Jug.* 92.7), and the only approach road was narrow and precipitous. Hurling stones and fire, the defenders easily destroyed the shelters that concealed Marius' advancing troops. However, by chance, a Ligurian auxiliary collecting snails for his supper stumbled upon a hidden path to the rear of the fort. Immediately realising the potential for a ruse, Marius sent a small task force of trumpeters and centurions by this alternative route, while he himself launched a full-scale frontal assault under a *testudo* of shields, supported by catapults, archers and slingers. The defenders were so sure of their superiority that they had left the shelter of their walls; but the blasts of the trumpeters, when Marius' task force reached the rear of the fort, sent them into a panic, and they were easily defeated.

The sieges of the Italian Wars, 91–88 and 83–80 BC

Several towns were besieged during the Social War of the legitimate Roman government against rebel elements in Central Italy, who were seeking the rights of Roman citizenship. Unfortunately, there is no detailed account of the uprising, but hints are preserved especially by Appian and Diodorus Siculus. Events began at Asculum, where all the Romans in the town were slaughtered. Thereafter, rebels attacked the Roman colony at Aesernia, and beat off the consular army that attempted to relieve the town. Diodorus Siculus claims that the townsfolk expelled all of their slaves to reduce the number of hungry mouths, a measure which prominent Romans exploited to make their escape. As conditions worsened, the townsfolk resorted to eating dogs, and were finally starved into submission. Venafrum fell to treachery, Nola was betrayed, and the sack of Nuceria persuaded the neighbouring communities to capitulate and provide troops for the rebels.

Meanwhile, another rebel force besieged the colony of Alba Fucens and defeated the consul P. Rutilius Rufus, who was carried back to Rome 'dripping with blood' (Florus 2.6.12). His deputy, Cn. Pompeius Strabo, was besieged in Firmum, until a relieving force arrived and, together, they chased the rebels to Asculum, which in turn came under siege. Another rebel force, led by a native of Asculum, succeeded in breaking into the town, whereupon their commander ostentatiously committed suicide, despairing of his fellow townsmen's performance in the siege. The town fell to Roman forces a year later, in 89 BC.

Around the same time, L. Cornelius Sulla, who had served under Marius (usually ungraciously), marched against the town of Aeclanum. The townsfolk hoped to stall him, but his troops proceeded to pile firewood around the timber

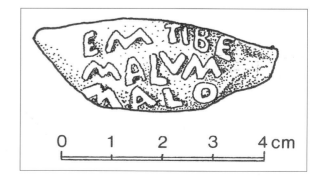

Dozens of lead sling bullets discovered in the vicinity of ancient Asculum (Ascoli Piceno in Italy) attest to the bitter fighting there, around 90 BC. Many are inscribed with the names of the competing generals and their legions. This one carries a message in vernacular Latin, to the effect of 'Take that!' (© Author)

The north wall of Pompeii, east of the Herculaneum Gate, survives up to 7m in height. The pock-marking visible here appears to have been caused by a barrage of missiles ranging from sling bullets to small-calibre *ballista* balls. These are likely to represent shots that fell short or were accidentally skewed during the siege of 89 BC, as Sulla's men directed their missiles at the timber gate or at the defenders on the battlements. (© M. Burns / Anglo-American Project in Pompeii)

fortifications and set them ablaze; the town promptly surrendered, but Sulla looted the place as a punishment. The details of how other towns, such as Canusium and Pompeii, fell to siege in 89/88 BC remain shadowy.

There was more siege warfare in 83 BC, when Sulla, returning from his campaigns in the east, was intercepted by the army of Marius' son (the old man had died in 86 BC, having stirred up Rome against Sulla). Sulla's battle-hardened legions drove the younger Marius' men to take shelter in Praeneste, which they proceeded to invest with a wall and ditch, to prevent any supplies getting through; even worse, as Sulla defeated successive relieving forces, he paraded the heads of their generals around the town to demoralise the besieged. When the townsfolk finally gave in, Marius hid in a tunnel and committed suicide.

Sulla and Mithridates, 88–85 BC

Sulla had been absent from Rome for four years, on account of the First Mithridatic War. In 88 BC, King Mithridates VI of Pontus overran Rome's possessions in Asia Minor; adding insult to injury, he humiliated the Roman commissioner there, M'. Aquillius, by parading him around on an ass before pouring molten gold down his throat to punish Rome's avarice. Mithridates then turned his attention to the wealthy trading city of Rhodes, whose inhabitants immediately strengthened their defences and 'erected war machines everywhere' (App., *Mith.* 24). An epic maritime siege ensued, but Mithridates' secret weapon, a fearsome contraption known as the *sambuca*, proved to be a disappointment when it collapsed under its own weight. It is likely that the fire, reportedly hurled down upon the machine by the goddess Isis, really came from Rhodian incendiary missiles. Meanwhile, the proficiency of the Rhodian fleet kept their Pontic aggressors from entering the harbour, and Mithridates withdrew in exasperation.

Sending his forces over to Greece, the king installed his favourite, Aristion, as despot of Athens, while his general Archelaus took charge of the port of Piraeus. By summer 87 BC, Sulla's five legions had arrived to besiege the divided Pontic forces. At Athens, Sulla was content to have his men contain the situation until he could personally capture the strategically important Piraeus; but the ladder parties that he threw at the walls in a lightning assault were repulsed. The artillery scholar Eric Marsden thought it an extremely optimistic attack, but he was perhaps influenced by Appian's exaggerated claim that the walls of Piraeus were 40 cubits (18.5m) high (App., *Mith.* 30). At 30 cubits (14m), the walls of Teichos, near Dyme, were thought to be unusually strong (Polyb. 4.83.4), and few city walls would have exceeded 10m. In any case, to attempt an escalade was a perfectly respectable tactic; after all, initial attacks on Carthage and Numantia, for example, had been based on escalade, and the Romans had often profited from such a bold approach.

Nevertheless, for a well-defended town to fall required either luck or a full-scale mechanised siege. Sulla decided upon the latter. After prevailing upon the neighbouring Greek towns to provide equipment, including catapults, he set his men the task of constructing siege machines; Plutarch makes the astonishing claim that ten thousand pairs of mules were in daily service, presumably hauling the raw materials (Plut., *Sulla* 12.2). Meanwhile, Sulla's legionaries threw up an embankment with earth, timber and masonry robbed from the ruined Long Walls that once linked the port to Athens. A story told centuries later, that one of Sulla's men was struck down by a thunderbolt while bringing up earth for the embankment, is perhaps a garbled report of the sling bullets which must have filled the air.

The *ballista* belonging to the Ermine Street Guard re-enactment group is the optimum size to launch stones weighing around 4 Roman pounds (1.3kg). Even such a lightweight catapult requires considerable space to operate efficiently. (© Ermine Street Guard)

LEFT **The largest of the stone missiles discovered during Schulten's excavations at Numantia (here labelled 1 and 3) have a diameter of 16cm, and weigh around 4kg (approx. 12 Roman pounds). Number 6, found in the town of Numantia, weighs 1.3kg; Schulten suggested that it had been shot from a 4lb *ballista*. Numbers 10 and 11, weighing 370g and 225g, were probably intended for throwing by hand. (A. Schulten, *Numantia: Die Ergebnisse der Ausgrabungen 1905–1912*, vol. III: *Die Lager des Scipio*, Munich 1927)**

Catapult arrowhead (length, 12cm; weight, 94g) found in the ditch of Caesar's small camp at Gergovia, during the 1996 excavations. (J. Ward; © ARAFA)

But Archelaus proved a formidable foe. Building up a siege tower opposite the Roman works and sending his men on midnight sorties to burn the Roman equipment, he even managed to undermine the embankment, and when Sulla sent sappers to tunnel their way into the town, they were intercepted underground and beaten back. The siege continued through the winter and into the following year. Finally, constant bombardment by Sulla's artillery disabled Archelaus' tower, and battering-rams positioned on the newly repaired embankment broke through; for good measure, the Romans also undermined a length of the town wall. However, although Sulla sent in troops in rotation, the Pontic garrison was still numerous enough to repulse his attacks.

All this time, Sulla had been intercepting supplies sent from Piraeus to relieve the beleaguered garrison of Athens. Consequently, hemmed in by Roman troops who had latterly cut a ditch all around the city, the inhabitants were weak from starvation; their only sustenance came from wild plants and boiled leather, and some had allegedly turned to cannibalism. When a poorly guarded stretch of wall came to Sulla's attention, he ordered a nocturnal escalade and unleashed his frustrated soldiers on the defenceless inhabitants. For this, he earned the disapproval of the later writer Pausanias, who commented that Sulla had been 'more savage than one would expect from a Roman' (Paus. 1.20.4). Pausanias must have known that it was standard practice to kill the males of sword-bearing age, but he perhaps expected the women and children to be sold into slavery, as Mummius had done at Corinth in 146 BC (Paus. 7.16.5). Instead, Sulla ordered a wholesale massacre, which Plutarch could only explain as retribution for the insults and obscenities that had been thrown at Sulla's wife from the walls. Returning to unfinished business at Piraeus, the Romans attacked the walls with such renewed energy that Archelaus was dumbfounded by their persistence, and evacuated the town by sea.

We have no Numantia for this period, no site where archaeology and literature combine to illuminate one another. Many sieges are known only from a brief notice in the sources. Frontinus mentions the capture of a town called Isaura in 75 BC by P. Servilius Vatia, who employed the well-worn stratagem of diverting the town's water supply (*Str.* 3.7.1). A fragment from Sallust's *Historiae* seems to describe the same event: it tells of townsfolk mounting a nocturnal sortie, in the mistaken belief that the Romans had abandoned their fortification; 'the ditches', writes Sallust, 'were half filled with the bodies of the slain' (Sall., *H.* 2 frg. 87). The chance find of an inscription in the wilds of Turkey not only confirmed the location of the town, but preserved the text of a dedication by Servilius, fulfilling a vow made to some deity for the successful outcome of the siege (AE 1977, 816).

Lucullus, Pompey and Mithridates, 74–71 BC

The two consuls of 74 BC, M. Aurelius Cotta and L. Licinius Lucullus, were keen to resume the war against Mithridates; the former lost no time in beginning naval operations, but was soon bottled up in Chalcedon and had to be rescued by his colleague.

From Chalcedon, Mithridates moved to Cyzicus, nowadays a peninsula but in antiquity an island connected to the mainland by a bridge. Plutarch records that 'Mithridates besieged the people of Cyzicus on both sides: by land, encompassing them with ten camps, and by sea, blocking up with ships the strait that separates the mainland from the town' (Plut., *Luc.* 9.3). Appian adds the detail that, 'as he possessed many soldiers, he pressed on with all the siege-works, walling off the [residential?] quarter with a double wall and surrounding the rest of the town with a ditch' (App., *Mith.* 73); embankments were also raised to carry battering rams. Meanwhile, the Pontic fleet brought siege machinery up to the walls (see Plate A), including a 100-cubit high (46m) wooden tower that carried catapults and missile troops. However, Mithridates was no more successful here than he had been at Rhodes 15 years earlier. All of his machines, 'the marvellous works of Niconides the Thessalian' (Plut., *Luc.* 10.2), were wrecked in a storm, and when poor sanitation brought disease to his siege camps Mithridates was finally persuaded to give up.

Lucullus' strategy of attrition, which Plutarch poetically rendered as 'thumping Mithridates in the belly' (Plut., *Luc.* 11.1), was unpopular with his legionaries, who were thereby denied the opportunity for plunder. Perhaps responding to this disaffection, Lucullus threw his troops enthusiastically at Themyscira; embankments were raised for siege towers, and tunnels were dug 'which were so large that, in them, a multitude could attack one another under the ground' (App., *Mith.* 78). However, the siege appears to have been abandoned when the defenders discovered the tunnels and inserted bears and other wild animals, including swarms of bees. Subsequent operations at wealthy Amisus (present-day Samsun on Turkey's Black Sea coast) took the form of repeated escalade, suggesting that Lucullus' troops had perhaps lost their appetite for digging full-scale siege-works. When a Roman assault finally caught the guards unawares, Callimachus, the king's deputy in Amisus, set fire to the town to cover his own flight, and succeeded in creating the maximum of confusion. Lucullus strove to save the place from destruction while his men rushed to ransack the burning buildings; next day, he is said to have wept as he surveyed the destruction, just as Scipio had done at Carthage (Plut., *Luc.* 19.4; cf. App., *Pun.* 132).

In the meantime, Cotta was engaged further west at Heraclea Pontica, where 'he devised machines, such as the tortoise, which he thought would be most terrifying to the besieged' (Memnon 34.1). But when his siege equipment failed to achieve results, spitefully he burned it and beheaded the engineers. The subsequent blockade provoked treachery in the starving town, and Mithridates' garrison commander opened the gates to the Romans. However, the victory almost turned sour, as the first Roman troops to enter seized the booty, denying a share to their comrades back in the camp; violent disagreement was avoided only by gathering all the valuables into a common pool and dividing them equitably. At Tigranocerta, where Lucullus finally tracked Mithridates down in 69 BC, the town was so rich that, besides whatever trinkets the individual soldiers could gather for themselves, each man received 800 drachmas from the store of booty (Plut., *Luc.* 29.3). And although mutiny in the ranks prevented Lucullus from landing the killer blow on Mithridates, he was permitted a triumph at Rome, embellished with 'the weapons of the enemy, being very numerous, and the royal siege machinery' (Plut., *Luc.* 37.2).

The *coup de grâce* was left to another of Sulla's protégés, Gnaeus Pompeius (the self-styled 'Pompey the Great'), before he moved on to Judaea to settle a succession crisis in 63 BC. Although the two quarrelling brothers, Aristobulus and Hyrcanus, agreed to abide by Pompey's arbitration, Aristobulus' followers seized Jerusalem and took refuge on the fortress-like Temple platform. Pompey approached from the north, and had an embankment constructed to fill the huge defensive ditch, 60ft deep and 260ft across (18 x 77m). Josephus claims that great progress was made on Sabbaths, when the Jews were forbidden to work and thus could not hinder the Romans (Joseph., *BJ* 1.146). Machines were requisitioned from Tyre to batter the wall and bombard the rebels, and after three months the Romans broke into the sacred Temple. Out of respect for the sanctity of the place, Pompey disallowed his troops from their usual plundering, but he himself could not resist the sacrilege of entering the Holy of Holies.

SIEGE WARFARE IN THE LATE REPUBLIC

Caesar's Gallic sieges, 57–51 BC

By the time of Caesar, the legions had long been noted for their skills in field engineering, best illustrated by the camp they traditionally entrenched after each day's march. Besieging armies are often mentioned building such a camp, or sometimes a pair of camps as Scipio had done at Numantia. However, the German scholar Willy Liebenam believed that he could discern a particular style of siegecraft that dispensed with all preparations in order to deliver a sudden and unexpected attack. Ironically, his inspiration came from the siege of Gomphi, a town in Greece which Caesar subjected to *repentina oppugnatio* ('violent assault') in 48 BC, when it shut its gates against him. But even here, the legionaries' first act was to build a camp outside the town, and their second was to construct ladders, shelters and screens (Caes., *BCiv.* 3.80); the assault, when it came, was certainly swift, but Caesar's preparations had been thorough. The situation at Cenabum (modern Orléans in France) four years earlier was very similar. Having arrived too late in the day to organise an attack, Caesar's troops settled down and pitched camp. However, when the townsfolk attempted to flee in the dark, the legionaries sprang into action; firing the town gates, no doubt to illuminate the chaotic scene, they set about looting and burning the place (Caes., *BGall.* 7.11).

No fewer than 17 sieges are known to have been prosecuted by Caesar himself, and many involved the constructional skills of his soldiers. Nowhere is this clearer than at Avaricum (modern Bourges), a town almost entirely surrounded by marshes, except to the south, where the only approach route was obstructed by a deep gully. When he besieged the town in 52 BC, Caesar had to construct a great embankment so that he could bring overwhelming numbers of men across the gully and up to the walls; in 25 days, the massive structure, 330ft wide (98m) and 80ft high (24m), was complete (see Plate B). A similarly breathtaking feat of engineering was accomplished in the following year at Uxellodunum (Puy d'Issolu), where Caesar ordered the construction of a 60ft (18m) embankment, from which a ten-storey artillery-armed siege tower could target the fresh-water spring that was sustaining the inhabitants and prolonging the siege.

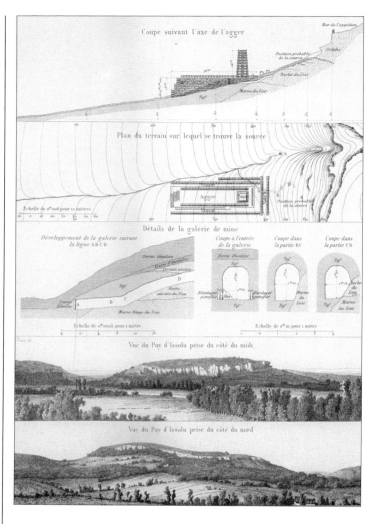

Coupe suivant l'axe de l'agger

Plan du terrain sur lequel se trouve la source

Détails de la galerie de mine

Développement de la galerie suivant la ligne A B C D

Coupe à l'entrée de la galerie

Coupe dans la partie BC

Coupe dans la partie CD

Vue du Puy d'Issolu prise du côté du midi

Vue du Puy d'Issolu prise du côté du nord

During Caesar's siege of Uxellodunum, the Gauls set fire to barrels filled with pitch, grease and wood-shavings, and rolled them down onto the Roman embankment. Napoléon III's investigations at Puy d'Issolu in 1865 led him to place the scene of this event on the western slopes, where he claimed to have found traces of burning. (Napoléon III, *Histoire de Jules César, II: Guerre des Gauls*, Paris 1866)

More usually, embankments served as runways along which heavy siege machinery could approach the walls of the besieged town. Sulla's embankment at Piraeus had fulfilled this function, as had Lucullus' at Themyscira and Pompey's at Jerusalem. Caesar's embankment at Noviodunum in 57 BC was of this sort: 'after the shelters were speedily brought up to the town, an embankment thrown up, and towers erected, the Gauls were amazed by the size of the works, whose like they had neither seen nor heard of before, and, perturbed by the speed of the Romans, they sent representatives to Caesar to discuss surrender' (Caes., *BGall.* 2.12). Similarly, 'when [the Atuatuci] saw a siege tower erected in the distance, after shelters had been brought up and an embankment constructed, they at first jeered from their walls and ridiculed why such a machine had been built so far away' (Caes., *BGall.* 2.30); but their scorn turned to alarm when the tower began its steady progress towards their walls, and they promptly sued for peace.

In all of these cases, for the chosen strategy to succeed, certain topographical features, such as the gully at Avaricum, made an embankment essential. Under different circumstances, an assault could be accomplished without one. For example, in 52 BC at Gergovia, atop a formidable hill accessible only from the south, Caesar decided to creep forward across the difficult terrain, consolidating ground as he went. From his initial encampment below and to the east of the hill, he seized the Roche Blanche, a small hill to the west, and 'carried a 12ft double ditch from the larger camp to the smaller, so that even individuals could pass back and forth, safe from a sudden attack of the enemy' (Caes., *BGall.* 7.36). Unfortunately, his plans were botched by the impetuosity of his troops, who were caught on disadvantageous terrain and repulsed; during the fighting withdrawal, no fewer than 46 centurions fell. In 1862, the archaeological remains of Caesar's earthworks were uncovered by Colonel Eugène Stoffel, during a programme of archaeological excavations sponsored by Napoléon III to provide information for his *Histoire de Jules César*. More recent work by the Association pour la recherche sur l'Age du Fer en Auvergne (ARAFA) has confirmed the existence of Caesar's two camps; but, at several points along the presumed course of the double ditch, only a single ditch was found, 1.70m wide and 1m deep, raising the possibility that the earthwork was not of uniform character over its entire length.

The earthworks at Gergovia were on a fairly small scale, and have more in common with field fortifications (for example, the ditches and artillery positions supporting the battle line at the Aisne in 57 BC; *BGall.* 2.8), than with siege-works. However, Caesar's general readiness to throw a rampart around an enemy town is surprising, for the technique of *periteichismos* practised by Scipio at Numantia had not been used (as far as we know) for 25 years. Its last proponent had been Sulla, at the siege of Praeneste, when he 'cut off the town at a great distance with a ditch and a wall' (App., *BCiv.* 1.88); four years earlier, at Athens, he had 'commanded the army to surround the town with a ditch, so that no one might secretly escape' (App., *Mith.* 38). The tactic presumably appealed to Caesar in the 50s, as it had to Sulla in the 80s. Perhaps such large-scale earth-moving exercises helped maintain discipline amid the tedium which sometimes accompanied siege warfare. Certainly, Plutarch claims that, when M. Licinius Crassus confined Spartacus' slave army in the toe of Italy in 71 BC by walling off the peninsula, part of his reasoning was 'in order to keep the soldiers busy' (Plut., *Crass.* 10.7).

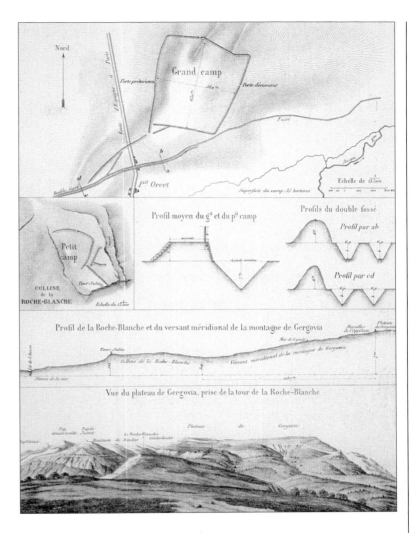

Details of Colonel Stoffel's excavations at Gergovie in 1862. Napoléon concluded that 'the communication between the great and little camps was composed of a parapet, formed by the earth thrown out of two adjacent ditches, each four feet in depth [1.2m] and six in breadth [1.77m], so that the breadth of the two together is twelve feet'. (Napoléon III, *Histoire de Jules César, II: Guerre des Gauls*, Paris 1866)

Equally, experienced soldiers like Sulla and Caesar must have appreciated the demoralising effect that encirclement had on an enemy. In 52 BC, after Caesar spent two days surrounding Vellaunodunum, 'on the third day, ambassadors were sent from the town to surrender' (Caes., *BGall.* 7.11). If they had not, it is likely that Caesar would have launched an assault. This was certainly the case in the following year at Uxellodunum. Prior to Caesar's arrival, his legate C. Caninius Rebilus planted three camps on the surrounding hills and 'proceeded to carry a rampart around the town' (*BGall.* 8.33); but it was Caesar's attack on their water supply that led to the townsfolk's surrender. Years earlier, in order to keep the Atuatuci within their walls while his embankment was under construction, Caesar had surrounded the town with 'a rampart 15,000 feet [4.4km] in circumference, with closely-spaced forts' (Caes., *BGall.* 2.30). Here, the investment was simply a prelude to an aggressive assault. Caesar's contemporary, the prolific letter-writer Cicero, claimed to have used a similarly aggressive technique when he besieged

Pindenissus in 51 BC; summarising the whole operation in a letter to his friend M. Porcius Cato, he wrote: 'I surrounded the town with a rampart and ditch; I penned it in with six forts and large camps; I attacked it with embankments, shelters and siege towers' (*Ad fam.* 15.4.10).

The siege of Alesia, 52 BC

Ironically, rather than Cicero's dynamic assault on Pindenissus, it is Caesar's blockade of Alesia that has often been taken to represent the Roman style of besieging. Topographically, Alesia, situated on the plateau of Mont Auxois, is strikingly similar to Numantia, and Caesar's chosen strategy was virtually identical to Scipio's; by maintaining a close blockade, he starved the defenders into submission. Caesar describes the sequence of events as follows: first, the army was encamped at convenient places; then 23 forts were constructed in a ring, to maintain a watch on the town; finally, siege lines were thrown around the site to complete the blockade. Colonel Stoffel's excavations between 1862 and 1865 were never published in full, as they were simply intended to corroborate Caesar's description of the siege for Napoléon's *Histoire de Jules César*, but parts of the siege-works have now been studied using modern archaeological techniques by a Franco-German team directed by Michel Reddé.

Napoléon decided on a sequence of eight camps, designated A to D, G to I, and K. There were sound archaeological reasons for placing A and B on the Montagne de Flavigny, and C on the Montagne de Bussy; indeed, in the 1860s, the ramparts of Camp B were apparently still standing, and a campaign of air photography between 1986 and 1995 revealed Camp C in amazing detail. However, there is little to recommend Napoléon's

ABOVE **North ditch of Caesar's large camp at Gergovia. The classic V-section of the ditch, approximately 1.1m wide and 0.5m deep, is visible in the side of the excavation trench. The hill of Gergovie can be seen in the background. (Y. Deberge; © ARAFA)**

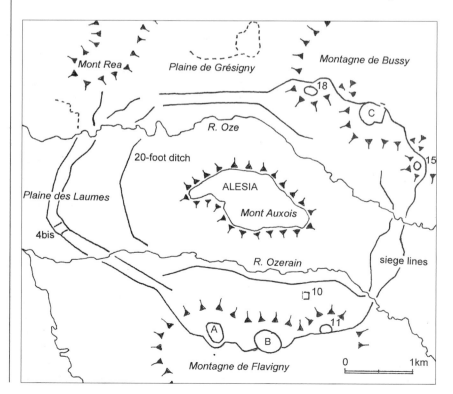

Plan of Alesia, showing features identified archaeologically or from aerial photography. Napoléon III's original scheme, identifying features by letter or number, has been retained for clarity. (© Author)

Aerial view of Mont Auxois (ancient Alesia) from the south, with the Montagne de Bussy behind. The course of the Ozerain can be seen in the foreground. (© Archéologie aérienne René Goguey)

placing of Camp D at the foot of Mont Réa. Stoffel could trace only a few disjointed lengths of ditch, but Napoléon conjured visions of the desperate defence of a camp here; he claimed that the hotchpotch of discarded weaponry and domestic refuse, which included pottery and millstones, 'would lead us to suppose that the Romans threw upon the assailants everything that came to hand'. Based on such feeble and circumstantial evidence, Camp D has long been doubted.

None of Napoléon's other camps demonstrates a close relationship with the siege-works. The enclosure on the Plaine de Grésigny, which he labelled Camp G, lies in an exposed position far beyond the siege lines, as do the features on the Plaine des Laumes which he proposed as Camps H, I and K. Indeed, recent excavations have shown that Camp I was post-Roman in date, a finding that recommends caution in assuming a Caesarian origin for the others.

Napoléon's 23 'redoubts' fare even worse, as even he admitted that only five actually existed, while the others had been pencilled in 'at the most convenient places' in a ring around Mont Auxois. Of the five genuine sites, only Napoléon's no. 10, on the northern slope of the Montagne de Flavigny, is convincing as one of Caesar's *castella*. No. 22, exposed on the heights of Mont Réa, is actually a prehistoric enclosure, and three others, situated on the Montagne de Flavigny (no. 11) and the Montagne de Bussy (nos. 15 and 18), are likely to have been among the camps which Caesar initially established.

Military operations were restricted on three sides of Mont Auxois by river valleys, but the open meadow of the Plaine des Laumes to the west offered a likely route, either for a massed eruption from the town or for the approach of a relieving force. So Caesar secured it with a ditch, allegedly 20ft (6m) wide with perpendicular sides. Stoffel located this feature, running in an arc from river to river, but its dimensions may

have been more modest than Caesar claimed; a section cut across it in 1996 revealed a flat-bottomed trench, some 3.1m wide and 1.3m deep.

Caesar described his main siege lines, 11 miles (16km) in circumference, as consisting of two ditches, the inner one filled with water, and a palisaded rampart with turrets every 80ft (24m) (see Plate C). Excavations in the 1990s on the Plaine des Laumes confirmed the broad outline of Caesar's scheme, while emphasising differences of detail. For example, the width of the innermost ditch, nearest the enemy, varied between 4m and 6.5m, and nowhere was it was found to be deeper than 1.5m; Caesar had specified 15ft wide by 15ft deep (4.5 x 4.5m). Five metres further out from the enemy lay a second ditch, consistently 2.7m wide but again never deeper than 1.5m. Surprisingly, 15m behind these, a third ditch was discovered, immediately fronting the rampart; it fluctuated between 1.1m and 3.2m wide and 0.8–1.4m deep. The rampart itself had been furnished with four-posted turrets at roughly 15m intervals. Minor differences of detail were discovered on the Plaine de Grésigny, where no third ditch was found, and traces of a wicker fence appeared in the strip between the first and second ditches.

Caesar claimed to have added further obstacles, 'so that the fortifications could be defended by a smaller number of troops' (*BGall.* 7.73): rows of five *cippi* ('gravestones'), or tree-trunks with sharpened

branches, sunk into 5ft (1.5m) ditches; eight rows of *lilia* ('lilies'), or sharpened stakes set vertically in 3ft (0.9m) pits, staggered in a quincunx pattern and concealed by brushwood; and *stimuli* ('spurs'), or barbed spikes fixed in foot-long (0.3m) lumps of wood and buried at random. Archaeological investigations on the Plaine des Laumes turned up subtle variations: six rows of small post-holes, only 1ft (0.3m) in diameter, filled the wide strip between the second and third ditches in a staggered formation, like Caesar's *lilia* but far smaller. And where the line turned around Mont Réa, although the excavators found only a single ditch, it was fronted by six or seven rows of small post-holes, again in the familiar staggered pattern.

Farther east, on the Plaine de Grésigny, the inner ditch was fronted by two parallel slots, 1.5m apart. If these are the foundation trenches for *cippi*, as the excavators suggested, then they represent another subtle departure from Caesar's description. Caesar stipulates 'rows of five', but it has never been clear whether he meant five ditches, or five lines of tree-trunks per ditch. Napoléon favoured the first interpretation, which has coloured all subsequent reconstructions of the Alesia siege-works, but the classicist Thomas Rice Holmes believed that the second interpretation better suited Caesar's Latin. Unfortunately, the trenches on the Plaine de Grésigny, each around 25cm wide and 20cm deep, are too small to have accommodated multiple rows of tree-trunks.

Having laid out one line of siege-works, Caesar then constructed another one, comprising 'similar fortifications of the same kind, facing the other way against the enemy outside' (*BGall.* 7.74). The excavations on the Plaine des Laumes found that the outer rampart was fronted by a 3.5m-wide ditch, an 8m gap, and a 5.7m-wide ditch. This line, too, incorporated obstacle fields between the ditches and beyond the outer ditch. The researcher and illustrator Peter Connolly has coined the term

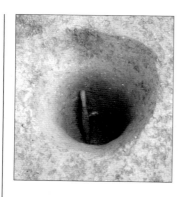

Iron point discovered *in situ* in one of Caesar's *lilia* ('lilies'), which formed an obstacle field in front of the ditch on the Plaine de Grésigny at Alesia. (© M. Reddé)

Schramm's reconstruction of the famous Ampurias catapult. The original iron spring-frame was discovered in 1912 at the ancient site of Emporion (Spain). It is thought to date from the later 2nd century BC, but similar machines were used from the days of Marius and Sulla right up to the Jewish War. (© D. Baatz)

'bicircumvallation' for double siege lines, one facing inwards and one facing outwards. Something similar had first appeared at Agrigentum in 262 BC and again at Capua in 212 BC,[7] and the arrangement was eminently sensible when attack might be expected from without, as well as from within. However, it must stand as testimony to the efficiency of successive Roman armies that they rarely found themselves in this position.

One feature of the siege-works at Alesia remains to be mentioned, namely the fortification discovered within the siege lines on the Plaine des Laumes; it has been named '4 bis', as it lies near the point where Napoléon placed *castellum* 4. Parallel ramparts were found to have closed off a compartment, roughly 100m square, between the inner and outer lines; each rampart was fronted by a ditch, 3.8m wide by 1.1m deep, and access to the resulting enclosure was via a gate, positioned where each rampart butted against the main siege lines. This seems a prime candidate for one of Caesar's forts, and others perhaps remain to be discovered in similar positions around the siege-works.

The sieges of the civil wars, 49–31 BC

Caesar's conquest of Gaul was substantially complete by 50 BC; alarmed by the increasing hostility of his erstwhile ally Pompey, he resolved to march on Rome. The ensuing struggle between the Caesarian and Pompeian factions spread across the Roman world and resulted in several well-known sieges. Most strikingly, Caesar continued to employ his familiar encircling technique. For example, arriving before Corfinium in 49 BC, his forces encamped on opposite sides of the town, before surrounding it with a rampart and forts; to prevent any escape, troops were deployed 'in a continuous ring of sentries and pickets, so that they touched each other and filled up the whole fortification' (*BCiv.* 1.21). In the event, the town was betrayed within seven days; much too early for us to decide whether Caesar planned to blockade it, as at Alesia, or take more active measures, as for example at the town of the Atuatuci.

A blockading strategy was certainly preferred on a few occasions. In 49 BC, as Pompey prepared to evacuate his troops from Italy using the port of Brundisium, Caesar attempted to blockade the harbour. Again, his legionaries showed their engineering skills, extending breakwaters from either shore and linking them with a substantial turreted pontoon bridge. But Pompey's heavy transport vessels were able to infiltrate the still-unfinished barrier, and he evacuated his troops just as Caesar entered the town by escalade. In the following year, Caesar caught Pompey on the Adriatic coast, and tried to prevent him from reaching his supply base at Dyrrachium (modern Durrës in Albania) by throwing a ring of earthworks around his position. Pompey's response was to begin his own ring of earthworks inside Caesar's, forcing his enemy to extend the outer line until it stretched for 17 miles (25km).

---

7. See Elite 121: *Ancient Siege Warfare: Persians, Greeks, Carthaginians and Romans 546–146 BC*, pp. 49 and 52.

'This was a new and extraordinary method of making war', writes Caesar, 'as much for the number of forts, as for the extent and size of the fortifications, and the whole manner of the blockade' (*BCiv.* 3.47). After frequent skirmishes, Pompey saw that Caesar was weakest in the south, where he had completed his ring by running twin ramparts, 600ft (175m) apart, down to the sea, but had not yet linked them along the coast. (Once completed, it would have resembled one end of Scipio's works at Carthage, in miniature, and is reminiscent of the compartment at Alesia.) A concerted amphibious assault by Pompey overwhelmed Caesar's fortifications, and he abandoned the operation.

Most interesting of all, though, is the case of Q. Cassius Longinus, Caesar's general in Spain. In 47 BC, having quarrelled with his quaestor, M. Claudius Marcellus, he encamped outside Ulia, hoping to benefit from the town's protection. However, both he and the town were hemmed in by Marcellus, whose siege-works were perhaps conceived as a miniature version of Alesia, as a substantial relief force is said to have been repulsed from the 'outer fortifications' (*BAlex.* 62). Caesar's governor in the province, M. Aemilius Lepidus, duly arrived to arbitrate, and ordered Marcellus to dismantle the siege-works.

Of course, not all sieges of this period were conceived as blockades. Caesar's attack on Ategua in 45 BC, for example, resembles his earlier operations at Vellaunodunum and Uxellodunum. The first stage was to encircle the Pompeian-occupied town with earthworks; this was then followed by the construction of an embankment, although work was hampered by the defenders' incendiary attacks. A section of wall was demolished, no doubt by battering ram (the text of the *Bellum Hispaniense* has been damaged at this point), but skirmishing continued around the siege-works, and Caesar was obliged to throw a ring of soldiers around the town. The siege finally ended, not with a storming assault, but with the surrender of the disheartened Ateguans.

A more spectacular example of aggressive siegecraft is provided by the attack on coastal Massilia by Caesar's deputy, C. Trebonius, in 49 BC.

De Folard's imaginative reconstruction of the siege of Massilia in 49 BC shows the besiegers' brick tower (left). However, it is clear from Caesar's account that the 18m-long gallery should extend from the tower right up to the town wall, giving complete protection to troops moving backwards and forwards. The wheeled shed is de Folard's own addition. (Author's collection)

He began to construct two embankments at different points on the landward side, but was severely hindered by the town's *ballistae*, which had allegedly been engineered to discharge 12ft (3.5m) iron-pointed spears instead of the usual rounded stone balls. The legionaries' standard wickerwork shelters could not stand up to such punishment, so Trebonius arranged for the workers to be protected by galleries made out of timber 1ft thick (30cm). In addition, he had a 30ft-square (9m) brick refuge built close to the town, so that the workers could shelter within its 5ft-thick (1.5m) walls; but he quickly realised how useful a tower would be in this location, and again exploited the legionaries' engineering skills to raise the structure, under constant threat of enemy fire, until it had six storeys. This opened up new possibilities, and Trebonius ordered a massive gallery to be built, 60ft (18m) long, stretching from the brick tower to the town wall.[8] Realising the danger posed by the gallery, the Massiliotes tipped blocks of masonry and blazing barrels of pitch onto it from the battlements above. But they were driven back by the artillery in the brick tower, and their improvised missiles were easily deflected by the gallery's 2ft-thick (60cm) gabled roof, with its coating of padded rawhide over clay. Then, concealed within the gallery, Trebonius' legionaries undermined the town wall, whereupon the townsfolk lost hope and surrendered.

Caesar's murder in 44 BC sparked off a new round of civil war involving his adopted son Octavian (the future emperor Augustus) and his erstwhile lieutenant M. Antonius (Shakespeare's Mark Antony). Again, a full range of siegecraft is in evidence. For example, late in 44 BC, Antony encircled Mutina (now Modena in northern Italy), where one of Caesar's murderers, Decimus Brutus, had taken refuge, but he was increasingly threatened by successive relieving forces and departed in the following spring. Octavian perhaps drew a lesson from Antony's failure. Late in 41 BC, when he trapped Antony's brother Lucius in Perusia (modern Perugia), he built an elaborate system of siege-works 'with two fronts, facing the besieged and any coming from outside' (App., *BCiv.* 5.33). Lucius was forced to surrender, after failing in his desperate attempts to break out. In 40 BC, when Brundisium (modern Brindisi in the heel of Italy) shut its gates against Antony, he cut off the town with a wall and ditch and summoned his siege machinery, but Octavian encamped nearby and the generals finally made peace with one another.

Armies operating in the eastern provinces were more ready to employ the techniques of Hellenistic siegecraft, either because the expertise was available there, or the sophisticated town defences demanded special measures. In 43 BC, another of Caesar's murderers, C. Cassius Longinus, built a wall across the neck of the Laodicea peninsula, trapping the governor of Syria, P. Cornelius Dolabella, in the town there. A naval defeat denied Dolabella an escape like that of Pompey from Brundisium, and Cassius proceeded to threaten the town wall with an embankment, but the town fell to betrayal. In the following year, while Cassius moved on to besiege Rhodes, his co-conspirator, M. Junius Brutus, assaulted Xanthus. The townsfolk had demolished the extramural buildings to deny their use to the besiegers as a source of

---

8. See New Vanguard 78: *Greek and Roman Siege Machinery 399 BC–AD 363*, pp. 35–6.

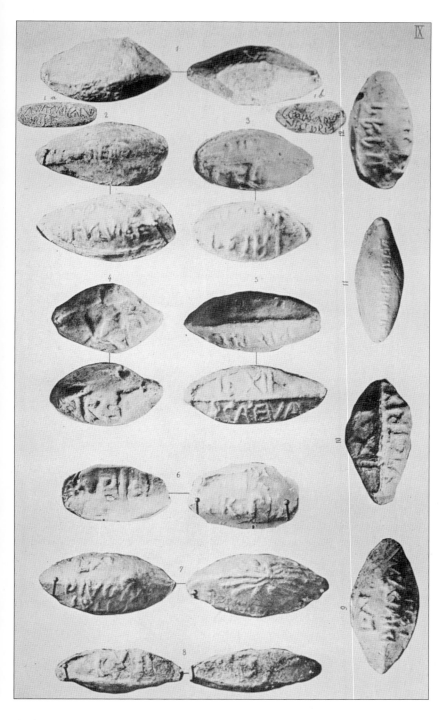

A selection of lead sling bullets from the siege of Perusia, 41/40 BC. The thunderbolt motif, which recurs on many bullets, can be seen on no. 7. Some bullets carry references to legions and personalities, such as no. 5, which names Caesar's redoubtable centurion Scaeva. Others carry insulting obscenities, such as no. 2, which names as its intended target the sexual organs of Antony's wife Fulvia. (C. Zangemeister, *Ephemeris Epigraphica* 6, Rome & Berlin, 1885)

timber; they took the further precaution of digging a 50ft (15m) defensive ditch, but Brutus' troops worked night and day to level out the terrain, and the Roman siege machinery soon arrived at the walls, where the townsfolk lost no time in setting fire to it. Plutarch claims that a change in the wind blew the flames back on the town, creating a conflagration (*Brut.* 30–31), but Appian writes that, when the Romans broke into the town, the inhabitants burned themselves and their possessions on bonfires (App., *BCiv.* 4.80). Whichever is true, the destruction of the town distressed Brutus, who had wanted only to extort money and troops.

A full mechanised assault was necessary in 37 BC, when Herod the Great, in alliance with Antony's general, C. Sosius, attempted to recapture Jerusalem from the renegade Antigonus. As in Pompey's siege of 63 BC, embankments were raised for the advance of siege towers and battering rams against the city's formidable defences, and the fortifications of the Temple platform were taken by escalade. Antony probably planned the same kind of operation when he arrived before the Parthian capital of Praaspa in 36 BC, but his 300 wagon-loads of siege machinery lagged behind and easily fell prey to a Parthian attack. Although he raised siege embankments, perhaps hoping to use them for an infantry assault as Caesar had done at Avaricum, he was eventually forced into an ignominious withdrawal, during which he lost around 20,000 legionaries.

Earthworks and siege machinery capture the imagination, but Roman armies had not lost their appetite for the simple brutality of the frontal assault. For example, in 43 BC, P. Cornelius Dolabella (destined to die months later in Laodicea) took the town of Smyrna in a classic *coup de main* under cover of night; when the general in charge, C. Trebonius, ordered his captors to take him to Dolabella, they replied that their general wished to see only Trebonius' head (App., *BCiv.* 3.26). In 35 BC, Octavian attempted a storming assault at Metulum, a town in present-day Croatia, raising embankments against the walls and throwing four boarding bridges across; but when three of them broke under the weight of the intense hand-to-hand fighting, the men refused to use the fourth, until Octavian himself ran out onto it. Although this one also broke, the townsfolk were sufficiently intimidated to surrender.

Rules of siegecraft?

Some scholars have argued that the Romans were bound by law to spare a town which surrendered, but this is nonsense. It is clear that writers like Sallust and Appian expected an honourable commander to show some degree of mercy, but Marius' treatment of Capsa in 107 BC shows that wider strategic requirements could take precedence. As a further example, while the Romans were engaged in settling a dynastic dispute in Judaea in 57 BC, the fortresses of Alexandrion, Hyrcania and Machaerus were surrendered, yet their defences were demolished, no doubt to prevent their use by rebels. More usually, the fate of a town rested simply on the mood of the commander, as with Sulla's sack of Aeclanum in 88 BC (see above, p. 14). Praeneste provides a more chilling example: Sulla certainly spared any Roman citizens among the population, but he had all the locals and the hated Samnites slaughtered, and plundered the town's wealth.

Another modern myth involves the battering ram as a symbolic initiator of the siege. It has been variously claimed that, once the battering commenced, there was no turning back; or that the option of surrender was rescinded as soon as the battering ram touched the wall. This notion is easily dispelled by reference to Octavian's siege of Metulum, where his initial battering assault was foiled by the construction of a new wall behind the breached wall; when his attempt to reach the new wall by boarding bridge, though unsuccessful, nevertheless alarmed the townsfolk, he was happy to accept their surrender. (In the event, they later reneged on the peace terms and had to be slaughtered.) But the idea of the battering ram as a point of no return derives from a misunderstanding of Caesar's ultimatum to the Atuatuci. He clearly implies that he will accept their surrender, only if they save him the trouble of bringing up his battering ram; far from obeying a fictional tenet of Roman law, he says that he is doing this 'rather because it is his habit [i.e., to be merciful] than because the Atuatuci might deserve it' (Caes., *BGall.* 2.32). Scholars have also pointed to Cicero's general plea, that mercy should be shown, not only to those who have been conquered, but also to those who have surrendered to avoid conquest, 'however much the ram struck their wall' (Cic., *Off.* 1.35). This is simply a rhetorical flourish, and should not be taken to prove that there was a rule, whereby mercy was never shown to those who surrendered during a battering attack.

SIEGE WARFARE DURING THE PRINCIPATE

When we turn to the Principate, the period of Roman history that covers the reigns of the emperors down to AD 284, few sieges are known in detail. Although Octavian (known, from 27 BC, as the emperor Augustus) continued to employ encircling tactics, for example at the mountain stronghold known as Mons Medullius, greater emphasis was again given to the storming assault. In AD 9, while campaigning in Dalmatia (an area now encompassing Croatia, Bosnia and Yugoslavia), the armies of Germanicus and the future emperor Tiberius stormed a succession of strongholds (see Plate E). At Splonum, there is the curious case of the cavalryman who terrified the defenders by knocking down a section of parapet with a stone; and at Raetinum, the townsfolk waited for the Romans to break in, before setting fire to the place and fleeing to safety.

A generation later, Cn. Domitius Corbulo, Nero's successful general (so successful that the emperor had him killed), was famous for saying that 'the pickaxe was the means of vanquishing the enemy' (Frontin., *Strat.* 4.7.2). Although he might seem to have been advising the reduction of strongholds by digging siege-works, Corbulo was probably advocating the protection of a campaigning army by carefully entrenching a camp each evening. His dynamic style of siegecraft is typified, not by earthworks, but by the kind of storming assault unleashed at Volandum in AD 58. Having set up a long-range barrage from catapults, slingers and stonethrowers, he sent one task force to undermine the defences, protected by a *testudo* shield-formation, while another moved ladders up to the wall; 'the attack was so energetic', writes the historian Tacitus, 'that within a third of the day the walls were stripped of their defenders, the barricades at the gates were overthrown, the fortifications were scaled and captured, and every adult was butchered' (*Ann.* 13.39). When his army subsequently arrived outside Artaxata, the townsfolk immediately surrendered, thereby saving their lives, although nothing could stop Corbulo demolishing their town.

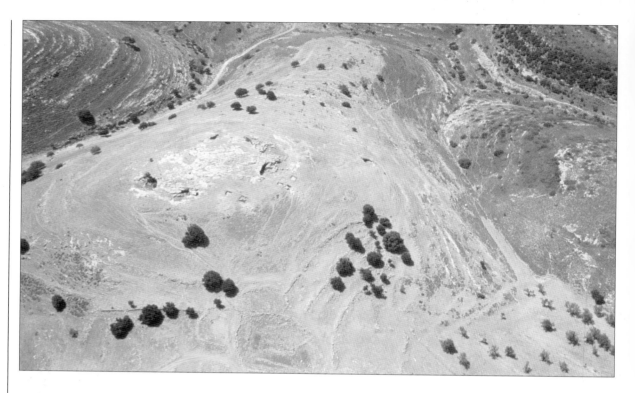

Aerial view of Yodefat (Israel), ancient Jotapata, looking south. Archaeological investigations on the northern slopes uncovered mortar and rubble which perhaps belonged to Vespasian's siege embankment. Quantities of arrowheads also came to light, along with two hobnails from the sole of a legionary's boot. (© M. Aviam)

The Jewish War, AD 66–74

The readiness of Roman armies to storm fortifications is again apparent from the events at such towns as Joppa, Gabara, Japha and Gerasa, during Rome's First Jewish War. Typically, once the defences were scaled, all males of sword-bearing age were slaughtered and the legionaries were given free rein to plunder and destroy. But these rapid actions have been overshadowed by the detailed accounts of more elaborate operations at Jotapata, Gamala and Jerusalem, and the spectacular archaeological remains at Masada.

At Jotapata in the early summer of AD 67, after the defenders had endured a week of assaults and had beaten each one back, the future emperor Vespasian decided to construct an embankment up to the walls. His intention, like Caesar's at Avaricum, was to enable his legionaries to storm across onto the battlements, but the defenders foiled his plan by heightening the town wall at this point. The historian Josephus, who was present as the defending general, records that Vespasian then brought up a battering ram, under cover of a missile barrage (see Plate D). But, although the wall was finally breached, the Roman attack was repulsed and Vespasian had no option but to increase the scale of the operation, yet again. This time, three 50ft (15m) iron-clad siege towers were constructed to overlook the town walls,[9] while the embankment was again heightened. Finally, writes Josephus, 'on the forty-seventh day, the Roman embankments overtopped the wall' (*BJ* 3.316); that night, the legionaries silently crossed over into the town and began the slaughter, sparing only the women and children to be sold into slavery.

(continued on page 41)

9. See New Vanguard 78: *Greek and Roman Siege Machinery 399 BC–AD 363*, plate F and p. 46 for a similar machine.

MITHRIDATES VI BESIEGES CYZICUS, 73 BC

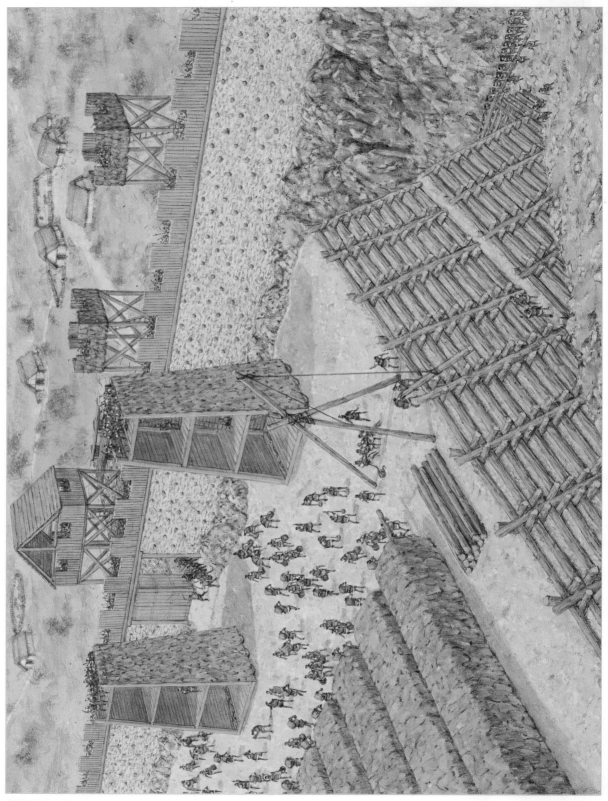

CAESAR'S SIEGE OF ALESIA, 52 BC

D VESPASIAN'S SIEGE OF JOTAPATA, AD 67

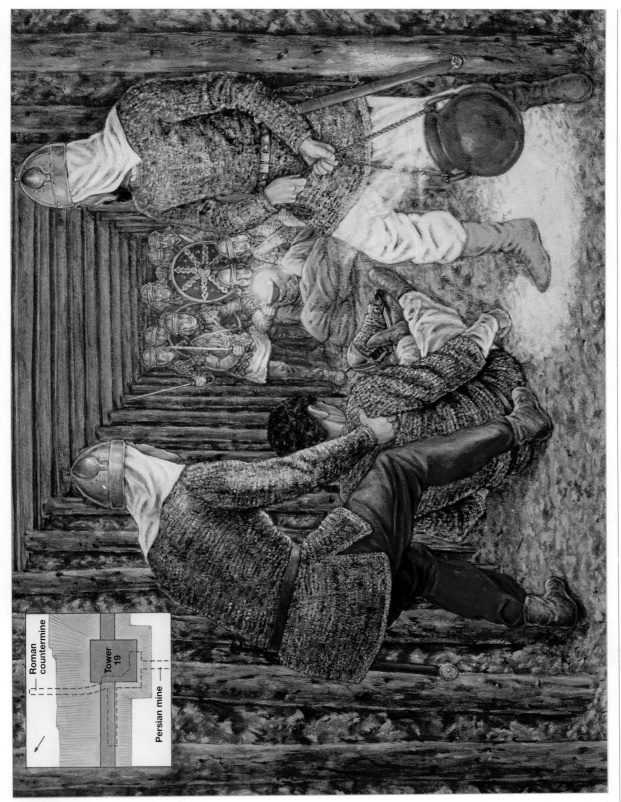

Roman countermine

Tower 19

Persian mine

PERSIAN MINING AT DURA EUROPOS, AD 256

F

The ancient site of Gamala (Israel), a steep-sided hill accessible only from the east, along a narrow neck of land (bottom right). The town wall was breached below the synagogue (bottom left). Over the years, archaeological work has turned up huge quantities of arrowheads and small *ballista* balls. (© Author)

Some months later, at Gamala, Vespasian again countered difficult terrain by building an embankment for battering rams. But when the legionaries eagerly burst into the town, they were hindered by the steep, narrow streets, and presented a static target for the missiles of the defenders, huddled high on the hillside. They withdrew as rapidly as possible, but a second attack succeeded, after one of the towers on the town wall was undermined. The legionaries set about their usual business, and according to Josephus (perhaps exaggerating only a little) 'blood, pouring downhill, flooded the whole town' (*BJ* 4.72).

The war reached its climax in AD 70 when, yet again, a Roman army arrived outside Jerusalem. Vespasian's son, Titus, orchestrated a full-scale siege, no doubt fully aware of previous Roman operations here. As Tacitus later commented, 'all the devices for conquering a town, known from the ancients or newly thought up, were assembled' (*Hist.* 5.13). Three embankments were constructed to carry battering rams against the outer wall, a new defence since the days of Pompey and Herod; a second wall was breached and taken; then two pairs of embankments were thrown up against the Temple platform. When one pair collapsed to undermining, and the other went up in flames, Titus briefly flirted with the idea of blockading the city, and had his men construct a 40-stade (7km) encircling wall, complete with 13 forts. As usual with major construction projects, the work gangs vied with one another to be first finished; 'the whole thing was built in three days', writes Josephus (*BJ* 5.509); 'for work worthy of months, the speed defied belief' (prompting one translator to comment wryly, 'indeed it does!'). But, as

41

so often in the past, no sooner was the encirclement complete than the assault began again in earnest. A new embankment carried rams up to the formidable Antonia fortress, which sat at the corner of the Temple platform; the demolition of the fortress opened up a broad ascent onto the platform itself, where the Temple was finally destroyed, despite Titus' protestations. In the days and weeks to follow, the looting and slaughter spread down into the city.

Although the fall of Jerusalem signalled the end of the war, rebels still held three of the fortified palaces originally built by Herod. At the first of these, Herodium, we know nothing of the siege. At the second, Machaerus in present-day Jordan, Josephus records that, 'after reconnoitring the vicinity, [the Roman commander Sextus Lucilius Bassus] decided to make his approach by heaping up [an embankment] in the eastern ravine, and set to work, hurrying to raise the embankment swiftly and thereby make the siege easy' (*BJ* 7.190). The archaeological remains show that, on the contrary, Bassus planned his assault from the west. It is on this side that the unfinished siege embankment can still be seen, and some way behind it a small camp of 0.18ha, which might have accommodated 100 or so men within its 2.9m-thick ramparts. Another nine or ten camps, most of them much smaller, are dotted around the site, linked by the disjointed lengths of a 3km circumvallation. However, it was not by assault that Bassus conquered the place, but by a ruse: having captured one of the rebels trying to attack the Roman lines, Bassus threatened to crucify him, whereupon the defenders surrendered.

The siege of Masada, AD 74

The third of Herod's palaces provided the setting for the most famous siege of the Jewish War, perhaps the best-known siege of all, at Masada; along with Numantia and Alesia, it offers that rarest of opportunities, the combining of historical narrative with archaeology. Bassus had died in office, so a new Roman commander, L. Flavius Silva, was sent out; the evidence of inscriptions suggests that he was given the Judaean command some time in AD 73, and must have arrived late in the year to

ABOVE LEFT **Scene from the Arch of Titus (Rome), showing the plunder from Jerusalem paraded in the triumph of AD 71. Garlanded men can be seen carrying placards (left and centre), probably describing the individual exhibits, and another carries the seven-branched candelabrum, or *menorah*, looted from the Temple. (© R. Cowan)**

ABOVE RIGHT **Scene from the Arch of Titus (Rome), showing the young Caesar (right) riding in a four-horse chariot, with winged Victory standing behind. On his return from the Jewish War in AD 71, Titus celebrated a joint triumph with his father, the reigning emperor Vespasian, thus emphasising the dynastic succession. (© R. Cowan)**

begin preparations for the siege. Like Scipio at Numantia, he 'immediately seized the whole area by establishing garrisons in the most suitable locations, threw up a wall in a ring around the whole fortress, so that it would not be easy for any of the besieged to escape, and distributed men to keep watch' (Joseph., *BJ* 7.275–6).

Studying aerial photographs of the site in 1929, the British archaeologist Christopher Hawkes believed that Silva had first encamped on the east side in Camp B, before transferring his legion to Camp F in the west. However, recognising a parallel with Numantia, Schulten realised that the two positions were complementary. Silva was simply following the standard practice of ensuring maximum visibility of the besieged fortress; in this respect, Camps B and F fulfil the same role as Castillejo and Dehesilla (or Peña Redonda) at Numantia, and Camps A (or B) and C at Alesia. Once the 4½km siege-wall was laid out, Camp C would have provided the manpower to patrol the eastern sector; at 0.43ha, it should be classified as a small fort but, lacking the fort's usual administrative buildings, it could have accommodated around 500 men. The similarly sized Camp E probably fulfilled the same role in the west. The smaller encampments, A and D in the east, G and H in the west, perhaps each held 200 to 300 men. Visitors to the site can still appreciate the observational role of tiny Camp H, whose position perched high on the southern cliffs parallels that of Cañal at Numantia.

Having encircled the enemy fortress, Silva began the next phase of assault by constructing an embankment. Again, these were tried and

ABOVE **Aerial view of Machaerus, looking east across the fortified palace (centre). In the foreground lies the main Roman camp (bottom right), and above it there are faint traces of the siege embankment mentioned by Josephus. (© D. L. Kennedy. APA98 / 30.10 / 17 May 1998)**

Camp C at Masada, viewed from the west. Schulten interpreted the rows of dry-stone structures inside the camp as barrack blocks, but the British archaeologist Sir Ian Richmond suggested that they were dwarf walls on which the soldiers pitched their tents to obtain cooler accommodation with less effort. (© Author)

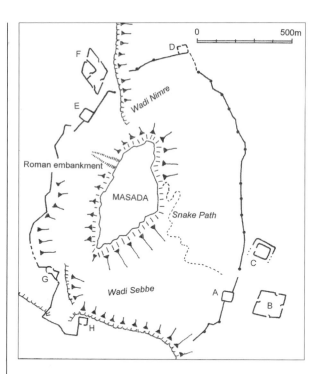

tested tactics, but the logistical feat seems incredible to the present-day visitor. Josephus says that Silva found only one place capable of supporting an embankment, namely *Leukē* ('the white place'), which he describes as a 'very broad rocky prominence which ran far out, 300 cubits [135m] below the height of Masada' (*BJ* 7.305). When Schulten explored the site in 1932, he was accompanied by General Adolf Lammerer, who suspected that the Romans had simply built the framework of their embankment onto an existing spur, jutting from the side of Masada. This has now been proven by the geologist Dan Gill, who has estimated that the bulk of the present-day ramp is a natural chalk outcrop, topped by 4–5m of compacted debris. The striking coloration of the chalk spur suggests that this was Josephus' *Leukē* (although its base lies 300 *feet* below the plateau, not 300 cubits).

'Ascending onto it and occupying it', writes Josephus, 'Silva ordered his army to pile up an embankment. Working eagerly and with many hands, the embankment was firmly raised up to 200 cubits [90m]. But he thought that it was neither firm enough nor sufficiently large to be a foundation for machinery, so a layer of large stones was fitted together on top, 50 cubits [22m] in breadth and height' (Joseph., *BJ* 7.306–7). No vestiges of this extra layer have ever been found. It is sometimes interpreted as a separate platform at the head of the embankment, but Silva's siege tower required a smooth

Plan of Masada, showing Flavius Silva's circumvallation with associated camps (labelled B and F) and forts. The security of the exposed eastern stretch was tightened by a series of towers. An earlier camp appears to underlie C, and may have belonged to an advanced reconnaissance party. (© Author)

The largest *ballista* used by Roman armies shot stones weighing 80 Roman pounds (1 talent, or 26kg). It was probably a machine of this size that, according to Josephus, smashed the battlements at Jotapata and knocked a man's head cleanly off his shoulders. The experimental machine depicted here was built for BBC Television; it is probably set at too high an angle for optimum shooting. (© A. Wilkins)

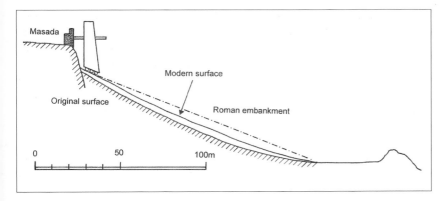

runway right up to the wall. Hawkes' suggestion of a stone causeway running up the crest of the embankment is the most plausible, but Josephus' measurements are problematic, unless his '200 cubits' refers to the original spur, and his '50 cubits' to the material piled on top by the Romans. However, Gill has suggested that, originally, this material averaged only 8m in thickness (6m along the crest, 10m on the sloping flanks), creating a smooth runway which, at its apex, fell 12m short of Masada's summit. Certainly, this would explain the extreme height which Josephus attributes to Silva's siege tower; but at 60 cubits (27m), the top 10m of the tower would still have overlooked the fortress battlements.

The iron-clad tower was reportedly equipped with catapults, and probably also held the battering ram which Silva finally deployed against the wall. However, it was well known that rams worked most successfully against stone fortifications, by dislodging individual blocks and shaking the wall apart, so when the Romans breached Masada's wall, the defenders threw up a timber-laced earthwork, against which the ram was powerless. As Josephus says, 'the blows of the machinery were weak from being directed against material which yielded and settled with the battering and became more solid' (*BJ* 7.314). Accordingly, Silva resorted to the age-old expedient of setting fire to the woodwork, but next day when his troops entered Masada they found that the defenders had committed mass suicide.

Modern scholars often imagine that this period was the high water mark of ancient siege warfare, although no obvious superiority can be discerned over the siegecraft of Sulla or Caesar. Marsden pointed to the 160 artillery pieces that Vespasian deployed at Jotapata as being a decisive factor, and it is true that, apart from their firepower, their psychological effect must have bolstered the army's performance while eroding the defenders' confidence. But the tactics

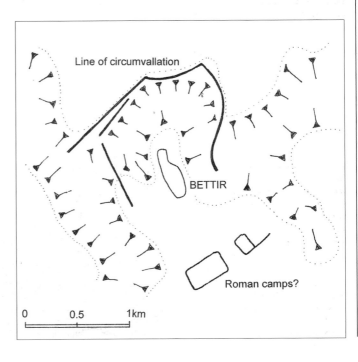

of the period can readily be paralleled from the sieges of earlier times. The massive preparations at Jotapata recall those of Caesar at Avaricum; the desperate street fighting in Gamala can be matched by Caesar's repulse from Gergovia; and at Masada, the circumvallation is a distant echo of Scipio's encirclement of Numantia, while Silva's tactics are the direct descendant of Cicero's at Pindenissus.

Sieges of the second century AD

Even during the periods of conquest that marked the reigns of emperors like Trajan (r. AD 97–117) and Septimius Severus (r. AD 193–211), reports of sieges are few and far between. This is not to say that no siege warfare occurred; only that the relevant historical reports have not survived. For example, Trajan's Column in Rome shows scenes of Dacian tribesmen attacking Roman fortifications, and Romans attacking Dacian hillforts, and the Column of Marcus Aurelius has scenes of legionaries looting German villages. It is particularly unfortunate that we lack a full description of the epic siege which gripped Byzantium between AD 193 and 195, as the defenders strove to repulse Severus' general, L. Marius Maximus.

Siege warfare in the East was overshadowed by three unsuccessful attempts on Hatra in present-day Iraq. First, Trajan attempted to capture the prosperous desert town in AD 117, but was almost shot while reconnoitring; poor weather and the attentions of troublesome insects forced his withdrawal. Then, campaigning in the same area 80 years later, Septimius Severus twice lost his siege machinery to the defenders' incendiary attacks (AD 198/199). On the second attempt, he managed to breach the outer wall,[10] but even 20 days in the stifling heat was too

Selection of sling stones, roughly 6cm in diameter and averaging 250g in weight, recovered from excavations at Tel Betar (ancient Bettir). Ballistic tests show that sling stones generally travelled farther than the lighter clay missiles, but fell far short of the smaller, denser lead variety. Over distances of around 80m, sling stones could be quite effective, although lacking the devastating armour-piercing potential of lead slugs. (© D. Ussishkin)

10. See New Vanguard 78: *Greek and Roman Siege Machinery 399 BC–AD 363*, plate G and p. 47.

Corpse discovered in Tunnel 1, behind Tower 19 at Dura Europos. Presumed to have been one of the besiegers, as he was facing the town when he fell on his back, he was perhaps cut down by Roman soldiers, intent on disrupting the Persian siege operations. He wears a ringmail coat, and a Persian-style helmet lay nearby. (© Yale University Art Gallery)

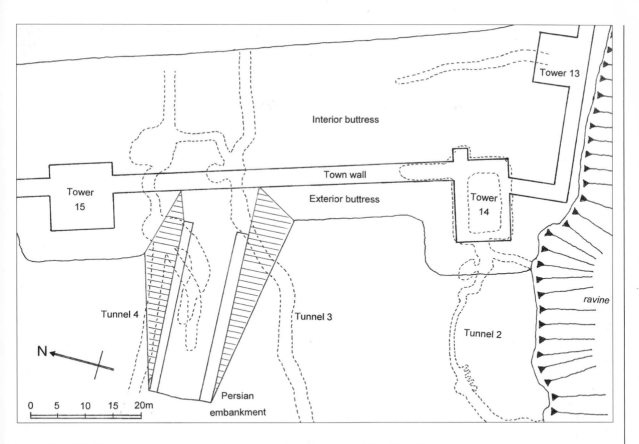

Labels on the plan: Tower 13, Interior buttress, Town wall, Tower 15, Exterior buttress, Tower 14, ravine, Tunnel 4, Tunnel 3, Tunnel 2, N, Persian embankment, 0 5 10 15 20m

long for his European veterans, who were already resentful after his execution of their favourite officer; Severus, like Trajan, had to acknowledge defeat at Hatra.

Sieges of the third century AD

Historical sources for warfare in the third century are even more fragmentary than for the second, and modern commentators shy away from discussion. Fortunately, archaeology has come to the rescue with two splendid siege sites, the first at Dura Europos in Syria and the second at Cremna in south-west Turkey.

Around AD 256, the Roman garrison occupying the desert town of Dura Europos began preparations to withstand an impending Persian attack. As the town was protected by natural ravines to the north, south and east, only the western side required attention; here, the Romans shored up the wall with great sloping banks of earth in front and behind. This had less to do with keeping siege machinery away from the walls, which could best have been achieved by digging wide ditches, and more to do with tackling undermining; for, if the walls were undermined, the makeshift buttresses would encourage slumping rather than total collapse. And, indeed, when the Persians successfully undermined Tower 19, midway along the town wall, only this emergency shoring preserved the defences. However, the subsequent abandonment of the town suggests that it was finally captured.

In the early 1930s, a Franco-American team of archaeologists discovered a Persian tunnel (Tunnel 1), measuring approximately 1.20m wide by

Plan of the Persian siege-works at Dura Europos. The convoluted arrangement of tunnels underneath the siege embankment would benefit from further archaeological investigation. The feature running north-west from Tower 13, once thought to be a Roman countermine, is probably a natural fissure. (© Author)

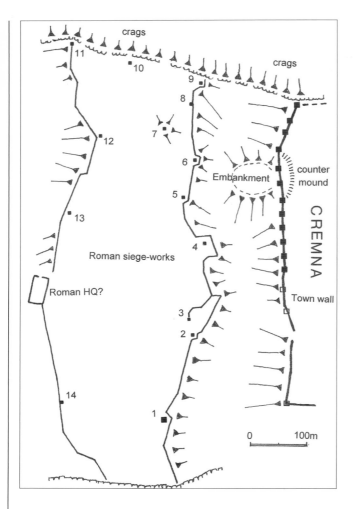

Plan of the siege-works at Cremna. The west wall of the town (right), built in Hellenistic times, faces a double line of siege-works across the broad natural valley that serves as the town's forward defence. (© Author)

1.75m high, passing under the corner of Tower 19 and turning to run beneath the town wall for about 15m. Following a tried and tested method, the Persian sappers must have shored up their work as they proceeded, so that the tower and adjacent curtain wall sat, not on bedrock, but on timber beams, which would subsequently be fired to bring down the fortifications.[11] Alerted to the Persian mining operations, perhaps by the sound of pick-axes or by the sight of the accumulating debris in the desert to the west, the Roman defenders dug their own countermine, intending to forestall the Persian plan (see Plate F). In the event, the mine was fired, but the Persians must have been dismayed to see that the tower still stood.

It was probably at this stage that they began to construct a siege embankment, some way to the south, beyond Tower 15. However, it seems that their work was hampered by missile fire from Tower 14, the southernmost tower, sitting just where the western desert wall turns and heads east along the brink of the southern ravine. To neutralise this threat, the Persians dug another tunnel (Tunnel 2), entering from the concealment of the ravine and skilfully directing its sinuous course right under the tower. Another smaller tunnel branched off, back to the ravine, perhaps as a ventilation shaft for the main combustion chamber.

Again, the massive buttressing of the wall prevented the tower's complete demolition, but its walls came apart as they sank into the mine.

We can only speculate as to the purpose of the curious knot of tunnels which passed underneath the siege embankment. The excavator, the Comte du Mesnil du Buisson, concluded, from his study of the pick-marks in the rock, that the two main tunnels were dug by the Persians. According to his scheme, as Tunnel 4 passed beneath the town wall, it was intercepted by the Romans, who then proceeded to burrow up into the embankment in the hope of destabilising it. That they succeeded, argued the Comte, is proven by the pronounced shelf which can be seen half-way along the embankment; furthermore, burnt areas exposed during its excavation showed that, in the Comte's opinion, two galleries had been dug and fired. In response, the Persians dug another tunnel (Tunnel 3) which, after passing under the town wall, turned north and broke into a large chamber where the Roman sappers were allegedly gathering. Finally, having neutralised the threat from Tunnel 4, the Persians used Tunnel 3 to invade the town, diverting attention from their colleagues storming up the partly collapsed embankment

11. See Elite 121: *Ancient Siege Warfare: Persians, Greeks, Carthaginians and Romans 546–146 BC*, figure on p. 60.

The so-called siege mound at Cremna, viewed from the north. The excavator interpreted it as an artillery platform, while acknowledging that it might eventually have carried a column of storm troops over the town wall. In fact, it bears all the hallmarks of a siege embankment, and was probably intended to bring a battering ram up to the wall. (© S. Mitchell)

outside. Although plausible, the entire scenario rests on archaeological evidence which is capable of more than one interpretation. Only further investigation will clarify the course of events.

The siege of Cremna in AD 278 is more straightforward. The historian Zosimus relates that, when a Roman army arrived in the area to deal with a bandit chieftain named Lydius, the latter took refuge in this well-fortified town, which was defended on three sides by impassable cliffs. His ploy to expel all those who could not bear arms backfired when the refugees were herded back into the town, so he tossed them over the cliffs. Lydius is said to have relied upon one man in particular, 'skilled in the construction of machines and capable of shooting missiles from machines with great accuracy' (Zos. 1.70); when this artilleryman was punished for uncharacteristically missing his aim, he defected to the Romans and used his skill to shoot Lydius as he stood at an open window.

Zosimus gives no hint of the siege-works which came to light in the 1980s. Archaeologists found the remains of two parallel walls, roughly 250m apart, running across the only access route to the town; each was equipped with a system of turrets to assist in surveillance. As the only identifiable camp, a tiny 0.17ha enclosure, was tacked onto the outside of the outer line, the excavator believed that the siege-works formed a double wall facing the town. However, the orientation of the turrets shows that the western wall faced outwards in the manner of a bicircumvallation. The bulk of the troops would have operated in the area between the walls, like Scipio's army at Carthage.[12]

In time-honoured fashion, the construction of the siege lines was followed by preparations for assault. The most striking feature at Cremna is a huge artificial mound that spans the valley between the siege lines and the town wall. Although this has been interpreted as an artillery platform to enable a short-range barrage against the defences, it bears all the hallmarks of an unfinished siege embankment. No doubt a battering ram stood by, ready to roll forward when the remaining 20m gap was filled. Certainly, the response of the townsfolk was to thicken the town wall at this point with a 15m-deep counter-mound, obviously intended to

---

12. See Elite 121: *Ancient Siege Warfare: Persians, Greeks, Carthaginians and Romans 546–146 BC*, plate G and p. 63.

reinforce the curtain wall against the imminent battering attack. However, the assassination of Lydius must have led to the town's surrender.

THE ELEMENTS OF ROMAN SIEGECRAFT

The encampment

It was a matter of routine for a Roman army to fortify a camp after each day's march. Such camps are explicitly mentioned at several sieges, and it seems reasonable to suppose that, in most cases, the besieging general's first act was to provide secure accommodation for his men. Once the army had moved up for the siege, new encampments were required. The historical sources suggest that it was common to establish two camps in complementary positions, thus ensuring complete visual coverage of the enemy town. Often, supplementary guard posts were sited all around to keep a closer watch, in many cases linked by a continuous barrier of some kind. Vegetius, writing probably in the late 4th century, explains that 'besiegers make a ditch beyond missile range and furnish it not only with a rampart and palisade but also with turrets, so that they can withstand sorties from the town; they call such a siege-work a *loricula*' (*Epit. rei mil.* 4.28).

The Persian siege embankment at Dura Europos, viewed from the south-west. Excavations in the 1930s demonstrated that it was piled up between twin banks of mud brick, the right-hand one almost 2m thick, which perhaps continued above the level of the causeway to form side walls. Tower 15 can be seen on the left. (© M. C. Bishop)

The circumvallation

The term 'circumvallation' is not found in Latin literature. Ancient authors often use verbs with the prefix *circum* ('around') to indicate the surrounding of a town: for example, *circummunire*, to surround with a wall, or *circumvallare*, to surround with a rampart. But there was no special word to replicate the Greek *periteichismos*. At Alesia, Caesar refers simply to 'the Roman fortifications' (*BGall.* 7.78), and his forts at Dyrrachium were linked by 'continuous fortifications' (*BCiv.* 3.44).

Burnswark (Scotland), viewed from the west. The magnificent remains of two Roman camps can be seen, one on either side of the besieged hillfort. The siege is likely to have taken place in the later second century AD. (© G. D. B. Jones)

However, in a rare exception to the rule, he refers to the rampart and forts with which he invested Corfinium as a *circummunitio*, which literally means a 'surrounding fortification' (*BCiv.* 1.19). More usually, in order to indicate a circumvallation, writers employed a phrase such as Cicero's description of Pompey at Brundisium, 'penned in with ditch and rampart' (*Ad Att.* 9.12). And the author of the *Bellum Hispaniense* uses a different circumlocution, when he writes that 'Caesar besieged Ategua with fortifications, and began to draw arms around the town' (*BHisp.* 6).[13] In rare cases like Alesia, with its double siege lines, the second line was quite simply designated 'the outer fortifications' (*BGall.* 7.77).

In the 19th century, Napoléon III confused the issue by referring to Caesar's lines of investment, for example at the town of the Aduatuci, as 'contrevallations'. When he turned to Alesia, he applied the same term to the inner line, and dubbed the outer line the 'circonvallation'. This was the traditional vocabulary used by French military theorists to describe the double lines of earthworks common in 15th- and 16th-century siege warfare. However, Schulten deplored the French terminology, and proposed reversing the two terms used by Napoléon, so that the inner line (indeed the only line, where a single siege wall was used) was the *circumvallatio*, and the far more rarely used outer line was given the modern name of 'contravallation'. French scholars traditionally retain Napoléon's terminology for the site of Alesia, but its use elsewhere should be discouraged.

Interestingly, the author of the *Bellum Alexandrinum* refers to the siege-works at Ulia, which may have been of the bicircumvallation variety (above, p. 27), as both *munitiones* ('fortifications') and *opera* ('works'), in the same sentence (*BAlex.* 63). This is another problematic term, as the ancients drew no distinction between the building of earthworks and the building of machinery; both could happily be labelled 'works', and often

---

13. An individual length of wall was often called a *bracchium*, 'arm', or in Greek a *skelos*, 'leg'.

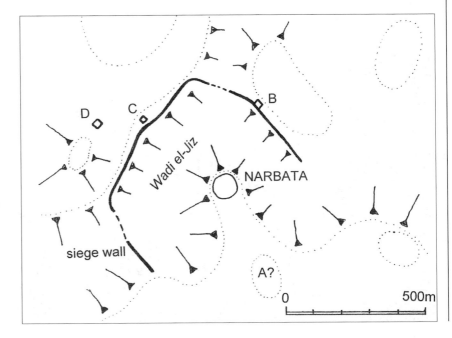

Plan of Narbata (Israel), where a Roman circumvallation has been recognised. The site exhibits several peculiarities, such as the small size of the three camps (marked B, C and D), only one of which is attached to the siege wall. The gaps in the north and south-west sectors may have been created by torrents in the Wadi el-Jiz, but the encirclement perhaps remained open to the south. Camp A is purely speculative. (© Author)

only the context indicates the author's intention. For example, writing about the siege of Ambracia in 189 BC, Livy draws a distinction between the *munimenta* 'by which the town was surrounded' and the *opera* 'which the consul prepared to move up to the walls' (Livy 38.5.1); the first are fortifications, and the second are machines. On the other hand, when Hirtius writes that, in 51 BC, Caninius constructed *opera* around Uxellodunum (*BGall.* 8.37), he is referring to the circumvallation.

The ditch and palisade was probably the most common form of barrier. Even when a solitary ditch is mentioned, as at Athens in 86 BC or Tigranocerta in 69 BC, the upcast material perhaps formed a low rampart. Of course, a ditch on its own, even a substantial one, may not seem a particularly secure barrier, but it would have served to apply the psychological pressure of containment. This was surely a major part of the strategy behind circumvallation. However, the Austrian scholar Georg Veith, overly influenced by Numantia and Alesia, concluded that Roman strategists must have favoured the blockade. The maxim attributed to Scipio Aemilianus, that only a reckless general would fight before there was any need, became misinterpreted as meaning that a good general took no risks; this in turn was taken as proof that the Romans preferred to starve an enemy into submission than risk shedding blood. Certainly, Schulten believed that the siege of Numantia (and, by extension, Alesia) embodied the famous strategy of *sedendo et cunctando* ('sitting and waiting'), whereby Q. Fabius Maximus had worn Hannibal down. Unfortunately, this has led many modern scholars to attribute an entirely imaginary policy of 'patient obstinacy and thoroughness' to Roman besiegers. But in doing so, they ignore the many instances of towns taken by sudden and bloody assault.

The siege embankment

As we have seen, there was often a requirement to pile up an embankment against the enemy wall, occasionally to elevate infantry for a massed attack across the battlements, but in most cases to facilitate the advance of wheeled machinery across rough terrain, or where the approach was impeded by ravines or gullies. It seems that all manner of material could be used in its construction; a Byzantine lexicon defines a siege embankment as 'a device of war erected from stones and timbers and heaped-up earth'. The prevalence of wood is confirmed by the many occasions on which defenders attempted to set them alight – for example,

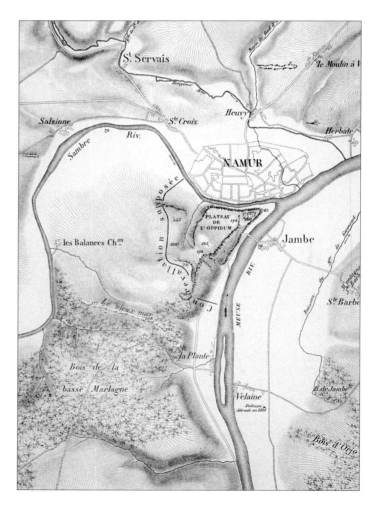

Napoléon located the town of the Atuatuci at Namur, and suggested a likely course for Caesar's siege rampart (here labelled 'contrevallation supposée'), but it is considerably shorter than the reported 15,000ft (4½km). (Napoléon III, *Histoire de Jules César, II: Guerre des Gauls*, Paris 1866)

Avaricum (see Plate B), Uxellodunum, Massilia, Jotapata (see Plate D), Jerusalem – and wood fragments were found in the embankment at Masada. The poet Lucan describes Trebonius' embankment at Massilia as earth and brushwood compressed by a timber framework at the sides.

Liebenam believed that, as a general rule, the siege embankment advanced, layer by layer, until it reached the top of the enemy wall. However, individual designs varied. At Avaricum, Caesar's troops still had to scale the wall, probably using ladders, whereas at Jotapata Vespasian was aiming for the battlements, before the defenders heightened the wall; having modified his tactics to allow a battering attack, Vespasian returned to his original plan and the embankment was again raised to overtop the walls. The topography at Gamala called for a different approach; here, the embankment simply evened out the rough and broken terrain so that machinery could be brought up to the wall. We read of defenders attempting to undermine embankments, which suggests that they could be substantial structures, even if they did not rise to battlement level. For example, at Piraeus, the walls stood on a 2m plinth of enormous squared blocks, so it is fair to assume that Sulla's embankment was intended to carry battering rams above this layer.

Liebenam's layer-by-layer approach is probably also mistaken. Stoffel's alternative suggestion is more attractive, that the work proceeded in huge steps, each gaining its maximum height before the next was begun. In this way, an unfinished embankment would not resemble Liebenam's low platform, which had achieved its desired length but not yet its target height; on the contrary, it would resemble Stoffel's mound, rising up in steps to its intended height, but still some way from the enemy wall. This is exactly what we find at Machaerus, where the steadily rising embankment was halted 50m short of its goal. Equally, the embankment at Cremna stops 20m short of the wall; its excessive width must have been caused by the spreading of the constituent earth and stones down into the valley.

Siege machinery

There was a long tradition of writing instructions for besiegers and the besieged, particularly concerning the construction of machinery. Under

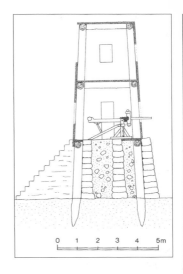

Schulten envisaged Scipio's towers at Numantia as two-storey, four-post structures, boarded on the outside. He interpreted the massive post-holes, found behind the 4m-wide siege-wall near Dehesilla, as marking the rear of the tower, and reasoned that the front legs must have been planted within the stone siege wall. (© Author, after Schulten)

North-east corner of Camp C at Alesia, viewed from the air. The camp ditch presents itself as a thick dark line, broken at the 12m-wide gateway. Two parallel lines of defences lie beyond the gateway, protecting it from outside in the manner of a *titulus*; also, the ditch can faintly be seen curving inwards, covering the gate on the inside. A smaller 'postern' can be seen to the right, where the ditch of the circumvallation meets the corner of the camp. (© Archéologie aérienne René Goguey)

View of Masada from the west. The white mass of the siege embankment is clearly visible climbing the side of the mountain. (© Author)

the patronage of the emperor Augustus, the architect-engineer Vitruvius devoted book 10 of his *De architectura* ('On Architecture') to machines of various sorts, some of which 'were invented as a protection against danger and a necessity for safety' (*De arch.* 10.10.1). Much the same ground was covered by Athenaeus, who wrote his *Peri mēchanēmatōn* ('On Machinery') for Augustus' nephew and son-in-law. But their texts concentrate on Hellenistic siege machines, and it is unclear how relevant these descriptions would have been to Augustan warfare. Certainly, the philosopher Onasander, whose *Stratēgikos* ('The General') was addressed to one of the consuls of AD 49, recommended that the siege commander should be familiar with a range of equipment, so that he could make an informed choice; but his own inclination seems to have been for the storming assault, delivered in waves, preferably where it would be least expected. Similarly, in his *Strategemata* ('Stratagems'), the high-ranking general and administrator Frontinus (a three-times consul,

During a visit to Masada in 1932, Schulten's companion, General Adolf Lammerer, realised that timbers protruding from the south side of the siege embankment must have belonged to the Roman structure's framework. (© D. Gill)

latterly as the emperor Trajan's colleague) entirely disregarded siege-works and machinery, in the belief that 'their invention was long since completed, and I see no substance for further perfection' (*Str.* 3.*praef.*).

Frontinus' judgement was premature. Besides the radical overhaul of artillery construction, generally dated to the period around AD 100,[14] we have the work of

14. See New Vanguard 89: *Greek and Roman Artillery 399 BC–AD 363*, plate E and pp. 37 & 45.

Apollodorus of Damascus, Trajan's architect and military engineer, who was evidently invited to produce designs for new siege machines. His text, entitled *Poliorkētika* ('Siegecraft'), assumes that a tribal hillfort is the focus of the siege, rather than a fortified town. First, he warns the reader against objects rolled downhill, a scenario that recalls the siege of Andetrium (see Plate E); but where Tiberius was prepared to persevere with a storming assault, Apollodorus recommends a system of banks and ditches to divert the hazardous boulders, tree trunks and wagons, along with sheds specially designed to deflect them.[15] Then he describes the sheds that will be needed, either to protect the legionaries during undermining work, or to carry the battering rams against a tower, a gate or the wall itself. The next section concerns the construction of a siege tower, followed by a novel system of interlocking ladders. He ends with a description of a battlemented raft for assaulting across a river. Some of the incidental elaborations are a little far-fetched, such as the addition of a torsion-powered truncheon to the end of a battering ram; although some of these are thought to have been added later by an enthusiastic editor, the core of Apollodorus' text provides a selection of machines which are 'effective, protective and safe, and that as far as possible are constructed out of easily obtained materials' (*praef.*1 [137.8–9]).

---

15. See New Vanguard 78: *Greek and Roman Siege Machinery 399 BC–AD 363*, plate E and pp. 45–6.

Aerial view of Machaerus, looking north. The remains of a siege embankment appear as an elongated hump on the left. (© D. L. Kennedy. APA98 / 29.37 / 17 May 1998)

A reconstruction of the ram tortoise described by Apollodorus of Damascus. The outer cladding of timber and wickerwork, covered with a fireproof layer of clay, has been omitted, so that the frame and undercarriage can be seen. (© P. Slisz)

EPILOGUE

The siege warfare of Rome's enemies

The story of siege warfare from 146 BC to AD 378 largely concerns Roman armies besieging non-Romans or other Roman armies. At the start of this period, Rome was the virtual ruler of the Mediterranean, having gradually absorbed the declining Hellenistic kingdoms of the east. Mithridates VI of Pontus was the last eastern potentate with the wealth and sophistication to field a siege train; even Herod the Great required Roman assistance to retake Jerusalem in 37 BC. In AD 51 when another Mithridates, this time the king of Armenia, was attacked by his neighbours from Iberia (present-day Georgia), he took refuge with the Roman garrison of Gorneae. This episode prompted Tacitus' disdainful comment, that 'there is nothing of which barbarians are so ignorant as machinery and the craft of besieging, but to us that aspect of warfare is well known' (*Ann.* 2.45).

It was common knowledge that the Parthians, who had inherited much of the old Seleucid territories in Iran, were equally inept at besieging. During the interminable game they played with Rome, each seeking to exert authority over the other by changing the ruler of Armenia, the emperor Nero propped up his nominee, Tigranes V, with a Roman garrison; the Parthians promptly besieged them in the royal city of Tigranocerta, but even using ladders and other machinery they failed. Their cavalry armies were more suited to the hit-and-run tactics that destroyed Antony's siege train in 36 BC.

The Germanic tribes are also generally charged with incompetence in siegecraft. Although Tacitus knew of two occasions on which German had besieged German, they relied on weight of numbers rather than technology or tactics. In AD 69, when a coalition of Germans, stiffened by renegade Batavian auxiliary troops, besieged the legionary camp at Vetera (Xanten in Germany), their makeshift siege machines were easily broken up by the defenders on the wall, and the arrival of a relieving force was enough to scare them off. Similarly, the Gauls who attacked the camp of Caesar's lieutenant, Q. Cicero, in 54 BC fled at the approach of Caesar's army. Astonishingly, during the preceding weeks, they had imitated the Caesarian practice of circumvallation and had erected a siege tower, under instruction from Roman prisoners. It is a salutary reminder that, even if the Romans had a peculiar affinity with siege warfare, they did not hold a monopoly on the construction and use of machinery, which could be achieved by non-Roman craftsmen and workers, given proper guidance.

Siege warfare in the fourth century

In AD 356, the future emperor Julian was wintering in a Gallic town with a small entourage when the Germanic Alamanni attacked, but they were unable to get through the locked gates. Ammianus Marcellinus, a participant in the military affairs of the day and a first-rate historian, says that, 'after forty days, the barbarians departed, grumbling that it had been futile and foolish to consider the siege of a town' (16.4.2). The Germans' continuing lack of success in siege warfare perhaps had more to do with their temperament than with any technological inferiority. A rebellious unit of Gothic auxiliaries, expelled from Hadrianopolis

Hatra, viewed from the north-east. The town is surrounded by a siege wall, which can be seen crossing the photo from left to right and running off into the distance. No associated camps or guard posts have been identified, and it may have been the work of Persian besiegers in AD 240. (© Author)

(present-day Edirne in Turkey) in AD 376, threatened to besiege the town, but were driven off by the defenders' arrows and sling stones. Two years later, following the disastrous battle in the neighbourhood, a Gothic horde again attempted a siege, but were entirely unable to make any headway (see Plate G).

Only with the rise of the Sasanian Persians did Rome encounter an enemy equally skilled in siegecraft. The scourge of the eastern provinces during the later third century, when they captured Dura Europos, Nisibis, and even Antioch, they continued to be a thorn in Rome's side. Ammianus describes the Persian siege of Amida in AD 359. The aggressors apparently used artillery and machines captured from the Roman garrison at Singara, and began piling up embankments under the protection of iron-clad siege towers. The fighting continued day after day, without either side gaining the advantage, until a huge earthen buttress which the defenders had built to strengthen their wall shifted forwards, breaching the defences and creating a bridge with the Persian embankment outside. Ammianus describes the horrific sequel, as the Persians sacked the town: 'armed and unarmed, irrespective of gender, were slaughtered like cattle' (19.8.4). The Persians enjoyed similar success in the following year at Singara and Bezabde with the same range of siege machinery and artillery.

Modern commentators often hold up the first century AD as a golden age of siege warfare, claiming that it declined thereafter. The belief is prevalent that later armies were less skilled in the besieging art, having forgotten how to construct an embankment or design a siege tower. This is patently false. In the fourth century, Roman and Persian armies alike

The Arch of Constantine, erected in Rome in AD 312, depicts troops attacking a town wall. Earlier in the year, Constantine had attacked Verona, held by his rival Maxentius' praetorian prefect, Ruricius Pompeianus. Rather than stand siege, Pompeianus decided to take his chances on the battlefield and was killed. (© R. Cowan)

achieved the same degree of sophistication as the armies of Caesar or Vespasian. For example, in AD 324, having trapped his rival Licinius in Byzantium, Constantine (later known as 'the Great') erected siege towers to overlook the walls and protect his men as they constructed an embankment; when the battering rams were ready to advance, Licinius fled and the townsfolk surrendered. Here, Constantine deployed the full range of devices familiar to earlier generations of besiegers.

Of course, availability of equipment was no guarantee of success. In AD 360, Constantius II, one of Constantine's sons, mounted a full-scale attack on Persian-occupied Bezabde in present-day Turkey. However, the Persians put up a more spirited defence than Constantine had met at Byzantium. First, Constantius' hopes of undermining the walls were crushed when the defenders dropped huge jars, millstones and column drums down onto the sappers' shelters. Then, after the Romans had thrown up an embankment and brought a giant battering ram up to the wall, the Persians unleashed a hail of fire-arrows; although the machine's fireproof coating kept it undamaged, it was effectively paralysed when the ram head became ensnared in a lasso. It was only with great difficulty that the Romans salvaged it, after the Persians had doused it in boiling pitch and pelted it with iron baskets of flaming brushwood. Finally, when the Persians surreptitiously set fire to the Roman embankment with hot coals, Constantius abandoned the enterprise in frustration.

Just as there was no noticeable superiority in the siege warfare of the early empire, so the later period brought no particular decline in Roman competence; although the conduct of a siege was theoretically influenced by the commander, it depended largely on the defensive capability of the town and the measures employed by its defenders. In a period that saw no major technological innovation, Julian's conduct at Maiozamalcha (AD 363), for example, where he raised embankments, deployed artillery and battered down the wall with rams, would have been entirely familiar to Scipio, Sulla and Caesar.

FURTHER READING

There are few general discussions of Roman siege warfare. Paul Bentley Kern's *Ancient Siege Warfare* (Souvenir Press, London, 1999) terminates at AD 70, and treats the period from 146 BC only summarily. The concise overview of 'Fortifications and siege warfare' in Peter Connolly's *Greece and Rome at War* (2nd edn, Greenhill Books, London, 1998) similarly takes as its limit the First Jewish Revolt, but Roger Tomlin appends a brief description of 'Siege warfare, 4th century'.

Although most of the historical sources can be found in the Loeb Classical Library, there is no English translation of Apollodorus.

SELECT BIBLIOGRAPHY

Baatz, D., *Bauten und Katapulte des römischen Heeres* (Franz Steiner, Stuttgart, 1994)

Berlin, A. M., & Overman, J. A. (eds.), *The First Jewish Revolt. Archaeology, history, and ideology* (Routledge, London, 2002) (pp. 121–33 on Yodefat; 134–53 on Gamla)

Connolly, P., *The Holy Land* (Oxford University Press, Oxford, 1999)

Deberge, Y., & Guichard, V., 'Nouvelles recherches sur les travaux césariens devant Gergovie (1995–1999)', in *Revue Archéologique du Centre de la France* 39 (2000), 83–111

Gill, D., 'Masada ramp was not a Roman engineering miracle', in *Biblical Archaeology Review* (Sept/Oct, 2001), 22–31 and 56–7

Jimeno Martínez, A., 'Numancia: campamentos romanos y cerco de Escipión', in *Archivo Español de Arqueologia* 75 (2002), 159–76

Liebenam, W., 'Festungskrieg (2)', in *Paulys Realencyclopädie* 6.2 (1909), 2236–2255

Marsden, E. W., *Greek and Roman Artillery. Historical Development* (Clarendon Press, Oxford, 1969)

Mesnil du Buisson, R. du, 'Les ouvrages du siège à Doura Europos', in *Mémoires de la Société Nationale des Antiquaires de France* 81 (1944), 5–60

Mitchell, S., *Cremna in Pisidia. An ancient city in peace and in war* (Duckworth, London, 1995)

Reddé, M., *et al.*, 'Fouilles et recherches nouvelles sur les travaux de César devant Alésia (1991–1994)', in *Bericht der Römisch-Germanischen Kommission* 76 (1995), 73–157

Schulten, A., 'Masada. Die Burg des Herodes und die römischen Lager', in *Zeitschrift des Deutschen Palästina-Vereins* 56 (1933), 1–185

Strobel, A., 'Das römische Belagerungswerk Machärus', in *Zeitschrift des Deutschen Palästina-Vereins* 90 (1974), 128–84

COLOUR PLATE COMMENTARY

A. MITHRIDATES VI BESIEGES CYZICUS, 73 BC
This scene depicts Mithridates' assault on Cyzicus from the sea. Pride of place among his siege machinery went to the shipborne tower, 'out of which, when they brought it up to the wall, a bridge sprang from under the machine' (App., *Mithr*. 73). This description calls to mind the machine known as the *sambuca*, which Mithridates employed 15 years earlier at Rhodes. Fortuitously, the historian Polybius describes in detail the version used by the Romans at Syracuse in 213 BC, perhaps the machine's debut, and that machine is the centrepiece of the scene.

Appian records that the defenders were driven back and four of Mithridates' soldiers managed to set foot on the battlements, but they were killed and the attack petered out. As nothing is known of the ancient walls of Cyzicus, a scheme of closed battlements and shuttered windows is suggested, as at Heraclea-by-Latmus. Such a fortification would have been difficult to capture by escalade, and might explain Mithridates' failure.

B. CAESAR'S SIEGE OF AVARICUM, 52 BC
This scene depicts the construction of a massive siege embankment, designed to level out the steeply shelving terrain outside Avaricum. Caesar's intention was to enable a massed infantry assault on the Gallic ramparts, but similar structures were used on other occasions to bring battering rams up to the walls of enemy towns. Two siege towers were erected, in order to command the battlements and provide the workers with covering fire, and the workers were protected by lines of shelters, as they moved backwards and forwards along the embankment.

The Gauls erected turrets on their ramparts opposite the embankment, as it drew ever closer; from there, they shot arrows and sling stones at the working legionaries, and pelted them with fire-hardened stakes and boulders. The work continued to completion, but Caesar then writes that 'the embankment was observed to be smoking, for the enemy had set fire beneath it via a tunnel' (*BGall*. 7.24). The blaze was quickly extinguished, but the story emphasises the fire risk posed by the timber content of the structure.

C. CAESAR'S SIEGE OF ALESIA, 52 BC
This scene depicts an assault on Caesar's inner line of siege-works. The Gauls had manufactured quantities of wickerwork panels, and equipped themselves with ladders and grappling hooks. The panels were for bridging the ditches, along with earth infilling; the ladders were for mounting the rampart, and the hooks for pulling down the Roman parapet. The assault was supported by Gallic slingers and archers. Caesar records that the Romans drove back the Gauls 'with slings throwing 1lb stones, as well as with stakes which had been distributed within the siege-works, and sling bullets', and adds that 'many missiles were discharged from the artillery' (*BGall*. 7.81). Many who survived the barrage trod on the spikes or stumbled into the lily pits in Caesar's obstacle zone, and the assault finally failed.

The most recent findings have been incorporated to give an accurate picture of Caesar's fortifications on the Plaine des Laumes; note, for example, the closely spaced turrets and the light fences screening parts of the inner ditch. Most interesting of all is the compartment between the two siege lines (known as '4 bis'), which has been reconstructed as a *castellum*, with tented accommodation for around half of a legionary cohort.

D. VESPASIAN'S SIEGE OF JOTAPATA, AD 67
This scene depicts a battering ram at its action station, at the head of the Roman siege embankment at Jotapata. The embankment was originally intended to elevate the legionaries to parapet level, but when the townsfolk cunningly heightened the wall to 20 cubits (9m), the Romans had no option but to break through, and the embankment became the runway for a battering ram. As Josephus comments, 'the Roman commander resorted to this plan, in his eagerness to take the town by storm' (*BJ* 3.218).

Catapults, archers and slingers maintained a constant barrage, so that the defenders would stay under cover and not interfere with the ramming work. But some, venturing onto the battlements to disrupt the operation, lowered sacks of chaff in front of the ram-head to deaden its blows; others rushed out with firebrands to set the Roman siege-works ablaze. Although one Jew managed to drop a boulder onto the ram and break its head off, the machine was soon repaired and the battering resumed.

The strong defences of Ceramus (Turkey), probably constructed in the later second century BC, seem never to have been tested in siege warfare. Sulla gifted the town to neighbouring Stratoniceia in 81 BC. (A. W. McNicoll, *Hellenistic Fortifications from the Aegean to the Euphrates*, Oxford, 1997. Reprinted by permission of Oxford University Press and Ms T. Winikoff)

Diorama of Caesar's siege-works at Avaricum, following the design proposed by General Verchère de Reffye, Napoléon III's artillery expert. His design was later criticised by the Comte du Mesnil du Buisson, fresh from his 1930s investigation of the Persian embankment at Dura Europos. Pointing out the fire risk, he likened de Reffye's design to a 'funeral pyre'. (© West Point Museum Collections, United States Military Academy)

E. TIBERIUS' SIEGE OF ANDETRIUM, AD 9

A band of tribesmen have taken up position outside their fortifications in order to hurl stones and other missiles at the attacking Romans who are struggling up the rugged slope. When the future emperor Tiberius was sent to Dalmatia to put down an uprising, he trapped Bato, the ringleader, in the hilltop fortress. Contemptuous of his barbarian adversaries, Tiberius ordered an uphill assault, while he watched from a platform. (It was usual for a general to observe in this way, so that any acts of bravery would be witnessed and rewarded.) The place was finally captured when a detachment of Romans made a wide detour and surprised the defenders by appearing on their flank.

The historian Cassius Dio reports that the tribesmen 'hurled down many stones, some from slings and some rolled down, and others let loose wheels, whole wagons full of rocks, and the circular chests native to that vicinity packed full of stones' (56.14). It was a common tactic, where the topography allowed it, for the besieged to roll heavy objects downhill; on other occasions, we hear of tree trunks and flaming barrels being used.

F. PERSIAN MINING AT DURA EUROPOS, AD 256

This scene depicts an underground encounter between Romans and Persians, both engaged in mining operations beneath the desert wall of Dura Europos. The archaeological evidence suggests that the Persians, having undermined Tower 19, had shored up the foundations ready to be fired, when the Roman defenders broke into their tunnel via a countermine. The Persians must have prevented the Romans from interfering with their mine, which was subsequently fired, causing the north-west corner of Tower 19 to subside noticeably.

Mystery surrounds the precise course of events. According to the interpretation followed here, the Persians succeeded in confining the conflict entirely within the Roman countermine, which archaeologists found intact. At some point, the Roman end of the countermine was sealed up, whether by the inhabitants, alarmed by the sounds of underground battle, or by accidental cave-in is not clear. Having repulsed the Roman tunnellers, the Persians sealed up their end also, leaving one of their number dead on the ground. The other corpses in the mine, a dozen or so soldiers huddled in the corner, perhaps choked on fumes, for the hardwood posts supporting the ceiling woodwork here showed signs of scorching.

G. GOTHS BESIEGE HADRIANOPOLIS, AD 378

The scene depicts the defence of a late Roman town against an attack by barbarian Goths, intent on looting the imperial treasure that they imagined lay within. The historian Ammianus Marcellinus describes the preparations of the townsfolk to

Roman legionaries assault an enemy wall. The famous *testudo* shield formation gave protection against missiles and objects thrown from above, represented here by a sword, a wheel and a firebrand. (E. Petersen, A. von Domaszewski & G. Calderini, *Die Marcus-Säule*, Munich, 1896)

stand siege: 'on the inside, the gates were blocked with large rocks, insecure walls were strengthened, and in order to shoot darts and stones from all sides artillery was deployed at suitable places' (31.15.6). The townsfolk joined the garrison in their efforts to repel the attackers, some of whom were preparing to scale the walls with ladders. Besides various missile weapons, the defenders dropped masonry and column drums over the battlements onto the Goths.

Details of the town defences are unknown, so it has been reconstructed according to the second-century remains of Xanten's south wall, with the addition of projecting gate towers. As the wallwalk would have been too narrow to accommodate the large one-armed catapult known as the *onager*, *ad hoc* thickening of the rampart backing is suggested. At the height of the drama a large *onager* hurled a huge stone into the Gothic horde, failing to crush anyone but terrifying the bystanders.

Tower 14 at Dura Europos, viewed from within the town. The Persian attackers successfully undermined the four walls causing the tower to come apart, thus preventing its use as a platform for catapults and archers. The buttress is a modern addition. (© M. C. Bishop)

INDEX

Figures in **bold** refer to illustrations.